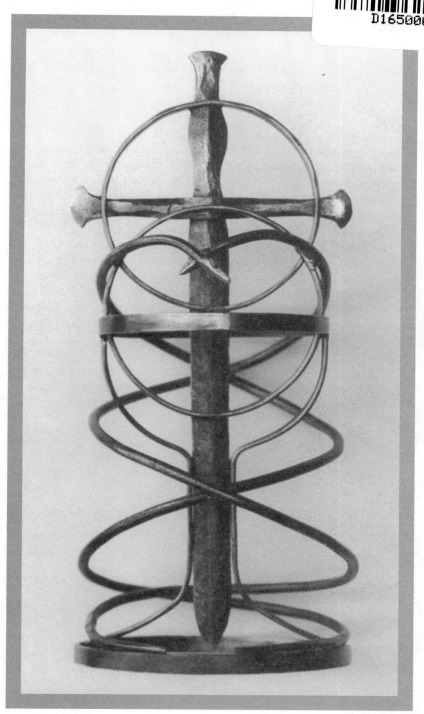

'CONVERGEN·CE'

'CONVERGENCE'

When I was commissioned recently by Richard and Geraldine De-Welles of Australia to create a sculpture to capture the combined energies of St Michael, the Holy Grail, the Vesica Piscis, and two twining serpents, I found it quite a challenge. It was while working in three dimensions with each element that I became aware that the energies had a natural tendency to 'live' together in dynamic balance, and I felt a strong affinity with the combined power as a symbol of how our many human energies, each retaining its own uniqueness, can blend to make a significant contribution to improving our quality of life.

The piece became a three-dimensional representation of what I was trying to express in words in the book, and with Gerry and Richard's kind permission I have used it as a visual image at the beginning.

Only eighteen inches high, it already seems to have its own unique energy pattern, and in the near future we hope to create a five-foot high version for the garden of their healing centre in Australia.

IT'S NOT TOO LATE

HAMISH MILLER

SPECIAL FIRST EDITION
OF 777 COPIES
BOOK NUMBER...557...

Hamish Miller.

Ba Russell

Penwith Press

First published in 1998 by
Penwith Press, Hayle,
Cornwall.

ISBN 0 9533316 0 1

Design by Evan Jones

Typeset and printed by
Penwell Limited,
Callington, Cornwall.

This book is dedicated to all those

who believe there's a lot more

to life than driving a Porsche.

It's also dedicated to my wonderful

partner Ba Russell, whose endless

patience, humour, critical courage,

editing, and dogged research

brought the plan

to fruition.

CONTENTS

LIST OF ILLUSTRATIONS

Illustrations by Stan Halfyard
and Hamish Miller

In the silence of deep night and in the
quiet still morning when the sun is
touching the hills, there is a great mystery.
It is there in all living things. If you sit
quietly under a tree you will feel the
ancient earth with its incomprehensible
mystery. On a still night when the stars are
clear and close, you will be aware of
expanding space and the mysterious order
of all things, of the immeasurable and of
nothing, of the movement of the dark hills
and the hoot of an owl. In that utter silence
of the mind this mystery expands without
time and space... Experience is the death
of that incommunicable mystery; ...to be
in communion with that, the mind, the
whole of you, must be at the same level, at
the same time, with the same intensity as
that which is called mysterious. This is
love. With this the whole mystery of the
universe is open.

From Krishnamurti's Journal

Chapter One

TRANSITION

"PITY WE WERE too late, chaps."

I became aware of the surgeon pulling off his mask and turning to his two young assistants.

He had told me with endearing candour the previous evening that most of my systems were failing and he'd like to have a look inside to see if anything could be done. By that time I was beyond arguing, and only too pleased that someone was willing to help. I asked him to do whatever he could.

The pre-med began in the morning and had been under way for some time when the edges of reality began to blur. The process seemed languid and gentle, and I was quite resigned to it all until I seemed to arrive, like a turkey on a trolley, in a vast kitchen with gleaming stainless steel ovens. I had an impression of a large, bearded Greek chef, smoking a cigar, and wearing a blue and white horizontally-striped jersey. He prodded me with professional interest and appeared to be concerned about my weight.

I suppose it must have been the anaesthetist.

I didn't seem to be able to communicate very well, and my last memory was of the urgency of letting him know that I was a trifle over thirteen stones — it seemed important at the time that at least I should be properly cooked.

"Pity we were too late."

The phrase hung in the air, taking a little time to register. Slowly I began to realise that I was somewhere outside the body on which they had been operating.

There was a dreamlike quality as I found myself looking down on the scene of the theatre. The 'ovens' were simple instrument trolleys and I could see myself lying peacefully centre stage. The players in this strange drama were preparing to pack up, and as the lights were switched out one by one the group who had been working on me chatted low-voiced for a few moments.

As they all turned to go, I felt the need to distance myself from what was happening. There was a momentarily sad recognition that the body which had served me so well for fifty-odd years was no longer capable of protecting and nurturing my being. I looked around, aware that my memories and senses were still functioning as they used to, but with a slightly detached added clarity which was intriguingly different.

Something was gently guiding me towards a quiet contemplation of this new state of being, and I relaxed in anticipation of what was to come.

The transition from one phase to the next was gradual and without fear ... no regret of unfinished business ... no tearful parting from people I loved, only a gentle floating upwards through a timeless zone of quiet patience and understanding. There was no coercion to do anything other than stay there for as long as I needed. Soft tendrils of compassion touched my senses while I drifted peacefully, apparently without aim.

Moments or aeons later I become conscious of an awakening curiosity to find out where I was. In leisured response, the surroundings slowly formed into the semblance of a tunnel. My discipline at an earlier time had been in engineering, and the sides took shape as curved rectangular pieces of polished metal with soft light shining through the spaces between the sections. There was a hazy feel of great distances behind the walls, and an impression of Vulcan-pounded rivets at the corners of the floating sheets. The light at one distant end of the tunnel was reassuring, its warmth comforting with a promise of more to come. I had left my body behind and my awareness was encapsulated in a burnished tube with gently rounded ends, invisibly suspended in the centre of the tunnel. The sense of acceptance, patience, love, understanding and a certain wry humour was all-pervading. Almost with a chuckle a voice somewhere inside said ...

"Don't worry, we really do know exactly how you feel."

The restricting concept of time disappeared. The tube was in limbo, ecstatically peaceful, nourished and cared for, with the life force within resting a while.

A QUIET LOOK BACK

There was nothing special in my origins. I think in hindsight I probably chose my parents because of my father's iron discipline and my mother's bubbling laughter. When she laughed she sometimes broke wind, and would go into paroxysms of helplessly irrepressible giggles. This usually made the problem ten times worse and inevitably triggered my father's thunderous glare of disapproval.

He was a dentist and, as was expected in those days, his behaviour had to be seen to be impeccable at all times. Mrs. Dale's Diary on the wireless at tea, the occasional game of bridge, and a few drams in Edinburgh on his Wednesday half-day were his only relaxations. His position in the mining town as a professional man made me a 'toff' at the local school, and very early on I learned to understand the huge gaps that even this minor social difference opened up. His punishments for my misdemeanours were actually few and far between, and were singularly effective because of that. With a solid, heavy hand, he defined lines of fair and caring behaviour, and I can't believe I'm much the worse for it.

A fierce Scot, he put himself through dental school in Edinburgh on a Carnegie grant. He spent the Meal Monday half-term holiday as it was originally intended, returning home to Caithness to collect enough rough oatmeal to keep him going for the rest of the term.

He was apoplectic about Manny Shinwell, the conscientious objector, subsequently becoming Minister of War, believed that there were no good Russians, and reckoned the English were not much better. Visibly shaken when my eldest sister Kathleen announced she was going to marry one, he thought throughout his life that she would have been much better off with one of the home brew. When my other sister Ivy did the same thing with a man from Bristol after meeting him on the wild Island of Skye, the precedent had already been set, and at least he thought the place they met was quite respectable. As he approached his four score years and ten, he affected a peculiar form of deafness when confronted by things with which he didn't agree, but could hear the top coming off a bottle of whisky at two hundred yards.

My mother quietly, and with disarming humour, guided us past the myriad rocks of growing up, supporting her man and providing the right background to his work, meanwhile contriving to give us a sense of adventure in our lives. She encouraged us to take up games, music, and to Join Things, although she didn't do any of these herself. A suggestion by me at the age of six that I'd like to be a blacksmith was met with a tolerant smile and a gentle but firm nudge in the direction of one of the professions or the Civil Service. As I was never able to establish exactly what a civil servant did, this potential career quickly disappeared from my agenda. She never said so, but she was well aware of the difficulties caused by the restrictive beliefs and prejudices of the small mid-Scottish town in which we lived, and kept well in the background. She had a wicked talent for mimicry, and had only to make the slightest nuance of expression or body language for us to know exactly who she was about to portray. My father seldom laughed out loud, but I can remember him, after some of her more outrageous impressions, helplessly wiping tears of laughter from his cheeks.

I joined the local Scouts, who introduced me to a mass of new things like maps and first aid, morse code and knots, tools for taking stones out of horses' hooves, tents and camping, and my first real rapport with growing plants, trees, animals, and the earth. It was an innocent and invaluable education which had a great influence on my future path.

It also led to an experience which was to shake me to the core, and raise questions which I hadn't dreamed of asking before.

I was about fourteen when a group of us decided to go off in the winter for a day or two to a Youth Hostel, and attempt to climb a mountain called The Cobbler, near Arrocher. One of our party had some minimal experience of climbing and we set off, skirting the loch, moving slowly up the slopes towards the ridge. I was totally ill-prepared, wearing smooth rubber-soled shoes, shorts, and had only one glove. With a great deal of puffing and blowing, sliding and slipping, we got to the exciting bit ... a three hundred foot climb out of a stone-covered corrie, thick with snow and ice, up to the col. The first part wasn't too difficult, but the last thirty feet or so was an almost vertical wall of ice formed by the fierce wind from the other side. We were roped together, and the leading climber cut some steps to enable us to scramble up the last few feet. As we hauled ourselves over the top, out of the shelter of the face, we were met by a whiteout of biting wind and blinding sleet, which took our breath and words howling back over the edge of the cliff. There was no shelter and we huddled, thumping ourselves and each other, trying to hold on to some semblance of warmth. When, after a few moments of triumph, the leader suggested we should start down, I was the first to volunteer. In his wisdom he had decided that we should unrope, and I started over the edge, feeling for the steps with my feet. The footholds were cut diagonally, and you had to change feet in each one to get down to the next. Inevitably, on the third one, my smooth rubber soles lost their grip and in a fear-ridden, frantically-clawing moment, I felt myself fall away from the icy face. I called out to my maker, aware that I was well beyond human help, and saw, as I spun down in apparent slow motion, a big ice-sculptured boulder fifty feet below me. I knew if I hit it with my head I would probably have very little chance of living through it. I heard, rather than felt, the crunch of my back striking the packed ice, catapulting me out with only the corrie below.

From a sheltered gully just under the lee of the col I watched, with a deep feeling of regret, this rag doll flailing down with explosions of snow and ice at intervals as it struck parts of the slope. I could see no possibility of its survival, and there were so many things I hadn't even begun to do. I saw quite clearly the headlines in the local paper — "Local Boy Killed on The Cobbler" — and could see older, wiser heads shaking at the stupidity of our venture.

An enveloping thump removed me from the gully, and I half opened my eyes to find myself in a white container, my body rigid and unresponsive. I thought that this might be part of the process of dying and waited for the next stage.

Slowly the sound of gurgling water underneath me made me aware that something else was happening. I opened my eyes again and realised that the white container was snow. With returning excitement, I found that I could move both sets of fingers and even wiggle both lots of toes. I couldn't move my back but looked up, breathed the air, and shouted with the joy of having survived. I found later that I had crashed through two or three inches of snow and ice covering the only stream in the corrie.

After what seemed like hours I managed to roll myself out of the stream bed and lay flat on my back on the snow bank. The faint sound of a shout came down from the little figures at the top of the ridge.

"Don't move till we get down!"

My response was in gloriously healing laughter at the thought of being able to move at all. I had taken only a few seconds to get to my place by the stream, but the party, gingerly finding another way, took an hour and a half. They helped me to the Hostel, another aching mile or so below, and the Warden, well experienced in these things, gave me treatment for frostbite and practically skinless hands and legs, and a fierce, unforgettable lecture on having the proper respect for natural things like mountains and the sea.

There is no doubt in my mind now that I went out of my body at the moment when I became convinced I was going to die. Five decades later I can remember with absolute clarity watching myself hurtling down the ice cliff, with the feeling of deep regret and sadness at the potential waste.

My first experience of working with growing things was with the Forestry Commission on the Braes of Balquidder. It involved staying at a Youth Hostel in Monachyle, getting up in the dark, cycling four miles to the Forestry Commission hut, climbing through the rain 700 feet up a mountain, finding a wee tree in the matted, two foot deep, soaking grass, clearing a space round it with a sickle, looking for the next one about six feet higher up the hill and doing

Two Exquisite Realities. Loch Voil.   H. MILLER

the same again. In the cold, wet conditions it was difficult to keep up my enthusiasm but something about the way the trees seemed to respond to the light was strangely satisfying. Planting and looking after them has given me rewarding pleasure ever since.

I had a nostalgic visit to the village some time ago and saw a fine spread of trees in the area where I had worked. For a moment I felt a great sense of pride, but realised that they were only about twenty years old. My wee trees must have been felled years before, and, in quiet contemplation of passing time, I turned and revelled in the incomparable beauty of Loch Voil on a sunny, still day, with its perfect reflections seeming to create two exquisite realities.

At school a number of Highers and Lowers reasonably easily attained with minimal homework gave me the erroneous idea that I could do the same at University. St. Andrews adjusted my sights to a new essence of being, improved my social life and golf no end, and led, after the first academically catastrophic year, to my walking into Perth Barracks to take up a not exactly voluntary career in the Army.

A suave Captain in the Education Corps assured me that with my background there would be no problem in getting into the Royal Engineers to help me further my career.

I looked forward to the posting with eager anticipation.

By some strange quirk of Army logic I soon found myself in an Infantry

Training Unit which specialised in teaching six ways to kill people with little bits of stick. Within a short time, by continually stretching us to absolute breaking point, then pushing us two stages further, they made us all disgustingly fit.

One of their favourite party tricks was ... all in the gym ... all given a number ... call out two numbers and make them box each other. I was immensely relieved the first time to find I was paired with Jimmy, my particular Glasgwegian mate who was roughly six feet tall and four feet wide. Many a pint had been downed in mutual condemnation of the instructors and I was confident of an easy passage.

To my astonishment and chagrin, he attacked with professional precision and enterprise, knocking the daylights out of me in no time flat. As he pulled me up from the floor, his grinning face registering smug pride and satisfaction at his handiwork, I opened one good eye and hissed at him through distorted mouth...

"I thought you were my mate!"

"Aye," he said, "but I'm no havin' 'lack of moral fibre' on ma sheet. It might affect ma demob."

Many an important lesson was learned in these days .... not understood at the time but woven into the matrix which would later have profound effects.

Finally, fully trained, fit and finely tuned for fighting, and with one stripe on my arm, my transfer to the Royal Engineers came through. Within hours I was on the train to Ripon in Yorkshire.

Training as a Deputy Military Mechanist (Electrical) was handled by superbly qualified and gifted Staff Sergeants, and I shortly gained one more stripe, an almost private cubicle in the hut spider, and an official R. E. issue bike whose speed and versatility enabled me to have two breakfasts, one very early, and another amongst the last of the weary-eyed, before everything was whipped away. After years of rationing it was bliss, and I have to confess that for a time I became eggbound. I understand that everybody in the billet was delighted that during this time I had my own cubicle.

Demobbed in Harrogate, I lost my brand new hat when I stuck my head out of the train window to greet Scotland again. My bird's-eye brown suit, however, lasted me for years.

I took up the threads of engineering again in Edinburgh, played rugby as fullback for Heriot Watt University, delved into the mysteries of industrial design, agonised over decisions about the most promising areas in which to specialise, and finally, having acquired a wife, set off to London to seek my fortune with GEC.

London was exciting at first ... so much energy and urgency. It took a couple of years to learn that working in a large company was not quite what I had anticipated. The very size creates a remoteness from human scale, and I saw with increasing concern more and more of my colleagues having their careers destroyed for reasons that had nothing to do with their capabilities.

The final crunch came when a smaller company was taken over in order to get the right hatchet man. When he moved in with his tame accountant, a staggering number of manufacturing bases, branches and departments were closed shortly after, on a strict basis of profitability, with no consideration for people. The human distress and anguish caused by this accepted business practice does not affect the bottom line, and there are rich pickings for those who are prepared to ignore even the most basic moral obligations.

I now had a son, and felt it necessary to have a little more control over my family's destiny. I had studied the design and manufacture of lighting fittings, and had a yen to broaden my creative base. As I believed that all designers should work at a practical level with the relevant materials before committing themselves to paper, I rented a small workshop where ideas could be transformed into products. Evenings and weekends were spent in acquiring the skill to make furniture and accessories, and I eventually sallied forth proudly, if naively, with my first candleholders to test the market. Some time later, bruised and battered by discerning and insulting buyers alike, I began to learn some of the tricks of the trade.

Libertys of Regent Street and Heals of Tottenham Court Road were at the forefront of furnishing and design in the mid fifties, and I found the patience and practical help from their buying and sales staff enormously encouraging.

I still treasure their first written orders as tokens of an important watershed in my life.

There followed a series of false starts, minor successes, failures and near misses, which are a natural progression in learning to run a business. The toll on family life during these times of stress is quite severe, and after a few years my wife decided she'd have a less chaotic future with someone else. All relationships, long or short, good or bad, are important for growth and experience. We both learned a great deal and there are no regrets on either side. There is an infinite pleasure now during summer holidays, when my son Roderick, his wife and my two grandchildren stay with us a while to experience the joys of Cornwall, and catch up with all that's happening in our lives. There is a specific joy, as all parents know, in seeing the little familiar behavioural characteristics in children which trigger memories from away back; and also, of course, in being ticked off by one's offspring in almost the same words as we used on them long ago.

Gradually the slippery foundations on the manufacturing side began to firm up, and the hard grounding in product design led to some long-term contracts which allowed our growing team to plan ahead. In a few years the company was employing over a hundred people and the financial rewards began to come in. I married again and to my great joy my second son Sean arrived at a time when things seemed to be progressing happily. He added a new dimension to our lives and it was an exciting and comfortable way of living in our fourteenth century timber-framed farmhouse in Sussex. I enjoyed the cut and thrust of designing products and running the business but in the background I gradually became aware of a feeling that there must be something more important to do with my life than make money.

During this time, on a visit to the West Country, I was walking in a quiet secluded valley near Trencrom Hill, when I heard a soft Cornish voice saying that the land beside the lane was being auctioned that afternoon. One of the gates was open and I followed a group through, not quite knowing why. It was a rugged area, full of bramble, bracken, gorse and huge granite boulders, with the occasional small stone-walled field grazed by horses. I sat on one of the stones and felt the all-pervading peace of being completely at home. My grandfather had crofted just such a place in Caithness, and I felt an irresistible pull towards this rough piece of land. I had time to walk only part of it before driving off to Penzance to the auction. I found myself nodding every time the auctioneer looked at me, and my rational mind rebelled at this madness with frenzied messages to stop and get out before it was too late. The hammer fell with excruciating slowness, and in a daze I went out into the sunlight. I had just bought twenty-six acres of Cornwall and, for the life of me, I didn't quite know why.

The negotiations stretched my finances considerably and I plunged back to work with renewed energy. Deep down I knew that my spontaneous acquisition would be of crucial importance at some later stage.

After a year or two of steady growth, I thought it would be pleasant to take my father round the works to show him what the wee shed had developed into. We walked through the busy cutting and welding shop, drilling and grinding sections, cleaning, spraying and packing areas, warehousing and offices, winding up in the boardroom. He'd hardly said a word the whole morning and, as I poured him a

Trencrom Hill

H. MILLER

drink, I asked him what he thought of it all. He took a deep draught of his whisky and soda, looked curiously at me and said ...

"It's not what you started out to do!"

It was a reference, of course, to my original choice of career as an electrical engineer. I felt like an errant schoolboy who'd let his dad down in an exam, and perhaps from that moment I began to question seriously the validity of the whole enterprise.

About this time my financial director went to New Zealand on an exciting new phase of his life, and sadly my marketing director died very suddenly from a heart attack. I had enjoyed working with both for a long time, and very much missed the occasional clashes and our many searching, stimulating discussions.

Recession was looming and we decided to carry on with the existing staff to keep overheads down. The pressures to survive increased but, although the work-load had trebled for me, I felt happy to handle whatever turned up and I looked forward to the time when, after a couple of years of good business, I could sell up and have time to do the things which had been niggling in my mind for years. On looking back I recognise that, like most people in business and finance, I had locked into the greed factor and I should have had the sense to quit while I was ahead.

By this time my wife and I had agreed to live apart after seventeen years of interesting but tumultuous living. She had been connected with the theatre most of her life and enjoyed bringing drama and challenge into every aspect of our lives. Conflicts of interest finally developed into a restricting brick wall of incompatibility for both of us. Our son, Sean, was just leaving school to study acting and directing, and we decided that, as we had nothing left in our relationship to give each other but distress, it would be more rewarding for each of us to go separate ways. Sean accepted our decision with mature understanding and has maintained a loving, caring, happy relationship with both of us all through the difficult times. He has inherited and improved his grandmother's talent for mimicry, and his gift of creating laughter and easy rapport through his impressions is a true blessing.

One Wednesday evening I came home after a fierce foursome of tennis and, while listening to the ominous news on the Falklands War, felt distinctly odd. I'd never been really ill in my life before and put it down to something I'd had for lunch. The following morning the pain in my stomach was so bad that I decided to have some time off for a rest. The endlessly long day gave me a chance, the first for a long time, to assess the value of what I was doing. Although my physical being was giving me major problems from all angles, my mental and spiritual bits were taking the opportunity to get messages through, which they had previously been unable to do. It was a transformational day, my mind wandering undisturbed by the usual daily dilemmas, except, of course, the bodily ones, which by this time were diverse and demanding. On the Friday I reluctantly decided to call the doctor and in a 'hanniclap' he whistled me into hospital by ambulance.

I was variously prodded, nurtured and drip-fed, while they tried hard to solve my problem without surgery. Unfortunately it didn't work, and I have to say that the National Health Service did a great job, pulling out all the stops to arrange an operation for the Sunday morning. I spent some time on the Saturday evening chatting quietly about life and death to a lovely Irish night-sister, and her gentle preparation for whatever was to come was inspirational.

Chapter Two

THE TUNNEL

THE TUBE FLOATED silently, untouched by all the forces in the universe.

Inside, the life force gently assimilated the recent hospital experience. The relative importance of events which before had caused so much turmoil was adjusted in the light of a newly evolving breadth of comprehension. Gradually, the great global problems emanating from social, emotional, religious and ethnic sources began to simplify, artificial boundaries disappearing as the futility of their existence became clear. Energies, which had for so long been dissipated on the absurdities created by human conditioning, began to direct themselves in a positive search for a clearer understanding of life and its meaning.

In the stillness, a slow dance of misty forms conjured visions of endless movement. Perceptions focussed to try to interpret their meaning, and softly an awareness of self returned, bringing with it a growing curiosity about the light at the end of the tunnel. In response there was a faintly discernible motion from the tube as it started to drift delicately along. Another stage of the journey had begun, and anticipation grew as it made its way silently on the ultimate pilgrimage. With infinite care it came to rest, still in shadow, but now very close to the source of light.

I have total recall of getting out of the tube feeling as if I was in the body of a small child, the symbol of innocence. Full of anticipation, excitement and awe, but totally unafraid, I walked towards the end of the tunnel.

Finger in mouth, I looked round the corner.

There was no specific source of light ... rather a transition from dark to bright diffused daylight. In front of me was a nebulous paved area, the colour of Carrara marble. I had an impression of soft, ever-changing, vaguely architectural outlines in the distance, with abstract shapes of clouds, the subdued colours forming the background to a sanctuary of utter peace and tranquillity. There were no human forms to be seen, but my recognition of the presence of benign and compassionate beings was so compelling, that I found myself moving towards them into the light.

At once my mind was allowed, with the greatest care, to have a glimpse of concepts we have no language to describe. A soft voice, heard from somewhere inside me, told me I was at the gateway to an altered level of being. I was welcome to join them, if I felt I had learned enough in my various lifetimes to contribute to, or even just to understand, their way of living. I had all the time in the universe, but I had to decide for myself whether I was ready to move on. My experiences from all sources and previous existences were made available to help in this judgement, and I was aware of being nurtured and supported in this time of absolute naked truth by total love and understanding. My unspoken questions were answered almost before they were formulated, and my mind was awakened to possibilities beyond dreams.

I lingered long in that wonderful timeless place, reluctant to do anything that might lead to my leaving. The concepts, momentarily revealed, involved working with thoughts and actions so far beyond my previous experience that, with regret, I realised I was truly incapable of contributing anything of value. I also had a clear impression that there were huge gaps in my knowledge which had to be filled before I stepped over.

My messages of thanks and my resolution to return to learn more were accepted by my hosts with quiet grace and almost a nod of approval. Their communications had been made with the greatest courtesy, reassuring humour and understanding, and as I moved towards the tunnel I knew, without a shadow of doubt, that I would be back. I left happily in that knowledge. As soon as I entered the tube, the 'child-form' disappeared, and I was again a simple life force, albeit with memory and purpose.

The return through the tunnel was swift.

In the distance the exit seemed to be barred by huge shards of broken glass, and as I hurtled towards it, I realised that a return to the physical state might be fairly traumatic. In the event the tube appeared to take the brunt of the shock, vanishing on impact, and I was suddenly aware of weight, pain, discomfort and a very faint voice calling ...

"Mr Miller ! Mr Miller ! Are you in there ?"

I was back in my body, lying in the hospital bed, surrounded by caring people.

I wanted to tell everyone where I had been and how wonderful it was, but sleep took over, and I lay blissfully unaware of the fundamental difference my experience would make to my future life.

Chapter Three

METAMORPHOSIS

RECUPERATION TIME in the hospital was a strange mixture of happiness in the glow of my recent experience, and concern to get my body back into shape for whatever lay ahead. I did as I was told, tramping up and down the ward in searing pain, feeling like an octopus with lots of flexible pipes sticking out of me. One of them was attached to a sort of mobile coatstand with three wheels and a mind of its own, which contrived to tie all my other tubes up in knots. I took a couple of hours to wash myself on the second day. Every movement was excruciating, but Sister was not impressed, and wanted the place tidied up in double-quick time. She made me cough deliberately and swept out smiling as I writhed in outraged agony.

"Better now than when you don't expect it," she called, disappearing down the ward.

She was quite right, of course. After that I was prepared for anything.

On the third day I had a visitor from the factory with a briefcase full of stuff which needed attention. When I glanced over the papers I was aware of the first murmurings of a significant change somewhere deep inside me. Things which had seemed so important a couple of weeks before were viewed from a different perspective, and I decided to allow myself enough time to recuperate before I made any decisions about the future.

My dear friend Ba Russell, a dedicated physiotherapist, with infectious enthusiasm had me walking correctly, further and further each day.

I began to see everything with new eyes and became aware that I was going through a crucial watershed in my life. Nature seemed incredibly beautiful. Colour was a bubbling joy. With heightened senses I looked at flowers as if for the first time, fascinated by their intricate design, smell, and touch. The appreciation of the simplest things ... sky, clouds, the restless sea, movement, being alive and breathing, became an exciting, sensual experience which rekindled my sense of wonder. The sound of wind in the trees, friendly footsteps approaching, the distant susurrus of traffic, all had an extra savour, while music stirred depths of emotion never previously touched.

I felt a sadness that many of the people I met were so wrapped up in trivia that these vitally important things were taken for granted.

The pure pleasure of being alive and truly responsive to the basic five senses is enough to make our time on earth worthwhile. If ethereal and spiritual dimensions are added, we can become a really unique species capable of communicating with the universe.

From this standpoint the business world took on a new focus and I had time to have a long clear look at what we were doing.

Barclays Bank were taking a bit of a pounding in the Force Ten gale of the '82 recession and I sought to consolidate our position by initiating a possible merger with another similar manufacturer. The process unleashed a series of interviews with a number of people at all levels in the business and financial world. With a few minor exceptions I have to say that the callous immorality of their reasoning was enough to make me recoil in dismay. There seems to be a serious malaise in the financial network, and it stems quite simply from the fact that people don't matter any more. A souffle of gigantic proportions has been created, a thick crust of computer networking data with absolutely nothing underneath, and a paradigm shift in the concept of sharing the earth's resources is absolutely vital for our evolution.

The simple act of giving freely generates a reward from the universe.

Negotiations with the bank were interesting. Gone were the friendly faces of the chaps we had dealt with for years, and in their place a bleak director, in formal morning dress, who talked at me from the other end of sixteen feet of rather splendid Georgian table. With clinical precision he outlined the bank's concerns. As I had been seriously ill, they could not really expect me to run the company to their satisfaction. Our perfectly viable plan to reduce overheads was not acceptable because it would take too long to take effect. I asked him about Maggie Thatcher's directive on television a short time previously, that manufacturing companies should be put into intensive care to enable them to ride the recession.

"May I make it clear, Mr Miller," he said, stiff-lipped, "the intensive care is for our money ... not yours."

For me the phrase encapsulated all that is wrong with current financial and business mores. The institutions are trapped in a system which world-wide requires each country to increase its Gross National Product year by year in order to survive. This is patently not sustainable, and in the name of progress, leads to an appalling waste of the earth's resources in producing mountains of cheap goods that nobody needs or wants.

One reason behind this frantic grubbing after an excess of material things is that, sadly, we have lost our belief in the continuity of our life cycles. An acceptance that our essence, after death, moves into a different and infinitely more mature form, would remove the urgency to grab everything we can in this short lifetime.

Immeasurably strengthened by my new and expanding set of values, I decided that my time in business was over and popped into the local bank to let them know. A few days later I walked into my office to tie up some loose ends, to find a diminutive Scotsman sitting in my chair. It seemed that he was from The Bank.

"I'm sorry, Mr Miller," he said, with rich rolling r's, and not a lot of preamble, "We can't afforrd you any more."

I wonder why it always seems to be a Glasgwegian who wields the knockout punch. It was not unexpected, of course, but the realisation that two decades of work and everything I possessed had just gone up in smoke was quite purifying. It was the fifth of November and I remember thinking that the management upstairs had a timely sense of humour.

For a short time I was disoriented, but soon became aware of an insistent call from Trencrom Hill, in Cornwall, to stop messing about and get down there. My previous hobby of blacksmithing came to fruition, initially as a means of earning a living, and subsequently as a powerful earthing balance when working in more esoteric fields.

As I shuffled off the old lifestyle, spending valuable, rewarding and recuperating time working on the land clearing gorse, bracken and bramble while fine-tuning the art of blacksmithing, I found I had much more time to think and respond to the more subtle energies from the earth.

I seemed to come across more and more interesting people. The gifted astrologer, Michael Colmer, opened a number of doors for me, one of which led me to find out more about healing. I had no idea how to start, and after joining the National Federation of Spiritual Healers, I sat like a lemon for

'Fine-tuning the art'   P. BROADHURST

weeks, watching my tutor working with people, and worrying that I hadn't the vaguest idea what to do. Thankfully, the time came when I began to work instinctively, and the break-through was a moment of pure joy.

I met Michael again later, and thought he was quite mad when he suggested that the earth needed healing just as much as people did. His quiet insistence on the importance of the earth's energy, and my subsequent work with it, has led me to some magical places.

Hand-forged Dowsing Rods   H. MILLER

A talk by Colin Bloy, the founder of the Fountain Group, on healing and earth energy lines introduced a new concept of human relationship with the cosmos. I was intensely intrigued by his demonstration of dowsing for earth energy and I asked him to point me towards a dowser with whom I could work.

"You can do it yourself," he said. "Anyone can do it."

I didn't believe him, of course, and left a bit disappointed that a door seemed to have closed.

The idea stayed on the back burner for a while, my mind toying with all that had been said. A number of 'coincidences' of chance meetings, of reference books falling open at the right page, of odd comments by complete strangers, led to the time when I found myself, with a strange sense of urgency, beating out a pair of iron rods on the anvil.

I set out for Trencrom Hill with mounting excitement, wondering if the new dowsing tools would show me if there was an energy connection between the ancient hill fort and St Michael's Mount a few miles to the south.

I shall never forget the awesome, joyous delight triggered by that first positive reaction of the rods. They moved, without doubt, of their own accord.

I knew that I had stepped out of another kind of darkness into light, as I had done once before.

Chapter Four

THE NEAR DEATH EXPERIENCE

THE REPERCUSSIONS of an out-of-the-body experience affect every part of one's being at a very deep level. Some of the effects are immediate and obvious, but many develop later, as fundamental internal transformations trigger different responses to everyday happenings.

Once back in my body I had found that there was still a slight tendency to resist change and to accept my old reactions to events around me. My friends, of course, just smiled knowingly, saying ...

"What else can you expect from an old Taurean?"

After fifty-odd years of life experience I had acquired lots of disjointed bits of knowledge, most of it pretty superficial. The trouble was that my interpretations of all this information, and my reactions to the various events, were manifestly influenced by family, school, religion, where I was born, and all the other factors which combine to make all of us the impossibly prejudiced creatures we are.

I found it strangely disconcerting at first to find that the old knee-jerk reactions to everyday occurrences no longer applied. There was a need for deeper consideration, a holding back of response, a compulsion to reappraise automatic answers which sprang from previous convictions. It was a time of rounding off the corners of intolerance and being aware of the bigotry which so often affects our behaviour.

A JOURNEY LESS FEARFUL

One of the most profound changes is the elimination of any need to live in fear. In that magical place of transition, you retain the full faculties of memory and experience outside the body, and feel a blissful surge of relief at the prospect of continuing your life in another form. In one glorious moment you know that there is no longer anything to be frightened of, nothing to lie about, and nothing to hide. It is an ecstatic state, stunning in its implications, and the perception of being able to exist in such a way is beyond most of us. Within our restrictive five senses and dense bodies, fear has been engrained in our psyche for millennia, and much of it has been induced in us subtly, but deliberately, by people amongst us whose purpose is to build manipulative power bases. These people, of necessity, can have no real perception of a life cycle which goes beyond our span on this earth.

Political, religious and financial power are geared to control, and the common weapon they all use is fear.

Think of the way that most people live.

There is fear of poverty, of illness, of authority, of what the neighbours would say, of a Vengeful God, of not being capable of loving, of competition from colleagues, of being excommunicated, of losing a job, of not providing adequately, of being alone, of losing one's money, of not being able to cope, of crime, of being a failure, of hospital, of dentist, of making one's own decisions, of change, of death ... the list is endless.

At this significant time when we are looking forward to starting a new century, many of us are feeling the need to stand quietly in our own peaceful space, questioning why we come to specific conclusions. Do the decisions feel good within us? Do they derive from long established prejudices? Are they influenced by one of the in-built fears? Are they made to placate friends, relations, neighbours, employers ... or can we now prepare to take hold of our lives and make decisions that feel right, based on concern and consideration for all other beings, including the animal, plant, mineral, and lower forms of life who share our planet? The decisions we make have a profound effect on everyone and everything around us, and we can develop the strength to accept our personal responsibility for them. The energy and positive emanations of love, humour and concern from our caring thought-forms are more powerful than the most strident newspaper headlines. They do not, of course, have the same immediate emotional impact, but have a permanence and potency far beyond the reach of any headline writer's dream.

Each one of us is capable of finding the special stillness and balance within ourselves. By looking inwards and recognising our prejudices, we can reach a still point of peace. From this point there is a way to communicate through advanced beings with our ultimate creator. The first effective step can be to start in a small way with our immediate surroundings.

I had a call the other day from someone who was having a terrible problem in sorting her life out. She had a number of self-inflicted religious and social wounds, and was fast on her way to becoming emotionally disturbed, caught in a web of the opposing needs of relations and friends, and trying to please them all. She went through a long list of things she was finding difficulty in handling, and which most of us would have solved without thinking, then went on to ask with some distress what she should do about problems happening on the other side of the world.

We had a long discussion which helped to rearrange some priorities.

Of course there's nothing wrong in sending thoughts to the larger issues ... the more minds involved, the bigger the chance that solutions will move into the global consciousness, and affect the decision-making process. But no one of us in isolation is capable of sorting out the world's dilemmas simply because, unless we have close and local immediate personal experience of the issues, our interpretations of the problems are influenced by whatever reports we see or read. But we can contribute a great deal if we get the scale right, concentrating in getting ourselves in shape first, and working on our own patch. On a local level you will immediately be guided to kindred spirits who will be operating on a similar wavelength, probably overlapping yours. The energy produced by a number of minds working together grows exponentially and can have a profound influence on our quality of life if it's applied in the right way.

One of the great difficulties we have to overcome in reaching a quiet balance is the influence of professional manipulators. They come in all shapes and sizes, and in all sorts of guises ... as politicians, religious zealots, media magnates, business tycoons, gurus, and hordes of others with lesser impact. Manipulation in this context can be something as apparently innocuous as persuading people to buy something they don't really want, because they are afraid to make the decision not to have it.

For example, has anyone really taken a serious look at the baseball hat?

Apart from the people who make, market and sell them, I mean?

Have any of the wearers actually seen what they look like?

"It's functional," they say.

So is a dustbin lid ... but up till now the marketing boys haven't caught on to this latest In Thing to wear!

Have they seen what they *look* like?

The power of advertising is extremely subtle, and uses the fear of not being able to keep up with your peers as a good reason to buy something. It will remain so until people start quietly making their own decisions, assert their independence, and quite simply learn to say...

"NO!"

Some years ago there was a particularly brilliant Italian designer who had a long history of success with his various racing cars. The drivers, of course, made a considerable difference in performance, but the fast and reliable vehicles were consistent winners. He was asked the secret of his success, and with an enigmatic smile he said,

"I just simplicate and add more lightness."

Perhaps we might consider this compelling thought in other aspects of our lifestyle. We have tied ourselves in the most complicated of tortuous knots in legal, social, business and political terms, and it seems we are afraid to ask questions in case we upset the status quo.

There are solutions available to us with even a minimal shift in perception. We can simplify our lives by clearing out unnecessary clutter from previous experiences, concentrating on the useful bits, and adding some light from our increased sensitivities. Light is simply understanding and awareness. Call it Christ-light if you like, but realise that all religions have the same glow within them, some a lot brighter than others.

Most of our information comes from television, newspapers and books. Fortunately we are gradually coming to terms with the fact that practically all we see and read is a misrepresentation of the truth. This can be through the natural prejudices of the writer or producer or, sadly, through deliberate campaigns to damage the credibility of people and organisations.

Prince Charles's innocent communication with plant life is treated with scorn by certain newspapers, as part of a calculated character assassination. It will be interesting to watch the desperate back-tracking of editorial slant, as an aware public learns more about our connections with all life forms, and decides that some newspapers are really not worth buying.

I had a large cheese plant in my healing room for years, and used it often to show the response to the energy coming from my hands. The visible reaction of the leaves, rising and bobbing as my hand passed near them, was a confirmation that at least the plant recognised the connection between us, and my victims were reassured that perhaps there might be something in it after all.

It's a rewarding and heartwarming experiment which you can try yourself. Hold a hand flat with your palm about ten to twenty millimetres above a large leaf, concentrate your mind on the plant, and with your inner voice say...

"You are beautiful."

If you say it simply, and with love, the leaf will try to move towards your hand in an endearing demonstration of the interconnectedness of all living beings. All plants react in the same way but it's easier to see the movement of those with a larger leaf.

It is a positive step towards the realisation that no living form exists in isolation, a practical way of showing that there may be many ways to connect with other and higher beings.

All of creation is linked, as part of an evolving process. An understanding of the simplicity of the ties throughout all nature means that no one need ever feel lonely again.

The effects from my experience have grown no less as time passes. It is a deep transition which has influenced my thinking on everything under the sun. The joyful acceptance that my essence goes on after death to an exciting new concept of living makes a huge difference in my everyday existence. The meeting with these benign and compassionate beings has taught me to look again at some of the things which control our lives on earth. From out there it's so much easier to get an eagle's overview of our problems, and perhaps in the following few chapters I may be able to convey some of the reactions I had to some of our more rigid behaviour patterns. Our 'evolved' society has developed terrible complications in our relationships, not only with partners but with neighbours, groups, tribes, cults, nations and the cosmos, most of them based on long established habits whose origins have been long forgotten ... the business and financial world has assumed an importance miles beyond its real value and is determinedly creating major health hazards for all of us ... our tunnel-visioned concepts of religion lead to appalling cruelty and suffering ... we are allowing our fragile bodies to be hammered from all directions by pollution and stressful living conditions ... and political and military establishments have not yet moved all that far from the ancient practice of claiming the best cave because you have the biggest club.

I am hugely optimistic now that subtle changes can be made to improve our lot on this earth. More people are tuning in and accepting the existence of higher beings. As we progress they will be delighted to provide the energy to transform us into happier, forward-looking, less self-indulgent humans with a sense of purpose in the universe.

Chapter Five

REWARDING RELATIONSHIPS

THE MIST HAD rolled back in the morning sun, cypress trees and monterey pines glistening in a kaleidoscope of changing colour. Brilliant aquamarine blue washed to creamy white as the sea swell broke on the rocks.

Wildcat Cove   H. MILLER

Wildcat Cove, south of Carmel in California, is quite stunningly beautiful, and my partner and I had spent an hour watching in silent appreciation the gentle, soft and joyously abandoned love play of a pair of sea otters.

Russian hunters almost exterminated these delightful creatures in the mid-eighteen hundreds for their superbly warm, luxurious fur coats, and they were thought to be extinct until rediscovered in the Big Sur area in 1938. There is a supreme innocence in the way they lie on their backs in the water on top of the kelp, arms folded or sometimes lazily scratching their heads in contemplation of the pure pleasure of living. Occasionally they rouse themselves, find some lunch in the shape of a shellfish, placing it on their chests and using a stone to break the shell open to get at the juicy bits.

The pair spent hours exploring each other, rolling slowly over and round, little arms encircling, stroking, teasing, moving gently through the water, sometimes

Sea Otters

together, sometimes just apart, but always in touch. The consummation was an expression of ecstatic selfless fusion and they floated quietly together with arms entwined.

What has happened to us humans?

It seems that over the last few hundred years we have been increasingly deprived of one of our greatest potentials for the development of our spiritual growth. The sexual union of two people, deeply and selflessly in love, without guilt and without fear, in innocent appreciation of each other can bring both as one fused being towards a spiritual awareness of the divine.

This mystical experience has an immense transitional power, which over the years has been recognised by those whose lives are involved in control. Religious leaders have devised many ways to intercede between people and their creator, and surely one of the most irresponsible and inexcusable is through the implication that sex is sinful.

I gather that the idea started somewhere back in the latter part of the fourth century with a chap called Augustine, who was the contemporary whizz-kid of the day on interpretations of what the Gospels and Jesus had actually said, and hence on the growth pattern of the Christian belief system. There was a bit of controversy about the accuracy of some of the Latin and Greek translations and Augustine carried a fair amount of sway with his versions. He was one of the first perpetrators of the myth that our species was created 'in sin'. I couldn't imagine quite how he got round to this from the old teachings until I chanced across his **Confessions** penned in later life.

According to him, when he was about sixteen years old he was '*dominated by the madness of raging lust*' and found that even with the greatest effort of will he couldn't control his erections. Don't we all have memories of feeling the sap rise, and looking forward with excitement to the day when this wonderful new feeling would reach fruition with a partner?

Not so with Augustine.

He felt so guilty about this powerful sexual arousal that his reasoning became a little suspect. He reckoned that our creator's gift to us of free will, free choice and personal liberty was liable to lead us into terrible trouble if we couldn't even use our will to control our sexual desires. Thundering loud and clear he preached that the great gifts had been despoiled by the first man and woman when they coupled in the Garden of Eden. It's almost inconceivable that the act of expressing their love for each other in the most natural and beautiful way could be construed as an affront to the creator. And as a punishment for this apparent misdemeanour we are all supposed to live our lives in bondage, obedience and fear for the rest of our time on earth.

Unfortunately he and his supporters had enough clout for this nonsense to be taken seriously. The problem of Jesus being born 'in sin' was neatly sidestepped by the astute and timely introduction of the idea of virgin birth, a wheeze taken from an old religion of a couple of thousand years before.

Over the centuries religious hierarchies have worked assiduously and successfully on the association of sex with sin, and have taken control, through fear, of something which should have remained an innocent joy for all of us. We can still hear, even today, certain members of The Cloth fulminating from the pulpit, with slightly sweaty brows ...

"Fornication is a mortal Sin!"

In these enlightened days it seems absurd that successive generations are still seriously restricted in their bodily pleasures by a notion that stems principally from one man's guilt about his personal problem.

We are still suffering from the artificial strictures of Victorian times, and their blatant sexual double standards. I recently saw a beautifully made musical box from that era, with an elegant pirouetting ballet dancer on the front for the ladies to watch, while behind, for the gentlemen, an erect penis pumped up and down in time to the music. The owner, I'm afraid, hadn't changed a lot from the top-hatted dandies who saw it when it was new, and giggled like a naughty schoolboy.

This sort of unhealthy interpretation of one of our most precious and delicate communicative functions has inevitably led to its cynical devaluation. Many newspapers and magazines depend on titillation of one kind or another to maintain their sales, and there is no doubt, at the moment, that we get the kind of printed stuff we deserve. Pornography is big business. Videos, computer software, and now the Internet are being used to peddle sex by people who see a quick profit in it, no matter what is being destroyed in the process.

Fifteen hundred years of manipulation and control of our sexual potential, initiated by people like Augustine and perpetuated by our society for all the wrong reasons, have had a profound effect on our relationships.

But people are now questioning this interference, and are beginning to make up their own minds about the subtle forces which attract some people and repel others. The marriage ceremony developed as a convenient way to gain official recognition for the consolidation of territory or property between a couple of powerful people or families. As the custom moved down towards the lower echelons of society and became an accepted commitment, the church moved in to impose its traditional control systems, implanting subtle fear and guilt as part of the ceremony. While it's a totally acceptable solemn and binding ritual for many people who are prepared to accept the strictures implied within it, I feel that one should be able to get married freely in the eyes of our creator by an equally serious affirmation of love and commitment anywhere in the great outdoors, not necessarily by a man of the cloth. Family life is going through changes which, at the moment, are rather disturbing but hopefully will develop towards a new and stronger togetherness. Couples of all ages are reappraising the quality of their lives. Enlightened thinking is generating more open and loving relationships, whether heterosexual, lesbian or homosexual, with a mutual bonding strong enough in its own right to overcome social, domestic and religious problems, denying the necessity for artificial controls.

THE VALUE OF BONDING

The advanced beings at the end of the tunnel treat relationships, in all the deeper levels, as essential liaisons to enhance spiritual growth. They see no particular virtue in perpetuating one which no longer provides that quality for both partners, because the vibrations which emanate from a non-nurturing pair have a detrimental effect on their immediate environment. Laughter, innocent enjoyment and togetherness release tensions and fears, and create the peaceful, calm conditions most likely to induce social and spiritual change.

Perhaps it may be too much to expect that one relationship in a lifetime can provide the breadth of experience needed by both parties. If it does work ... that's fine, and I feel that these couples are truly blessed, but there should be no social or religious stigma attached to anyone's decision to satisfy a genuine need to progress in a new alliance if the first is no longer based on love and mutual caring.

It's worth considering the virtues of having a number of close relationships during our time on earth, each as important as any other, but with a different purpose.

One youthful pairing could be as innocent as the sea otters, through ecstasy and mystical experience, to a rekindling of our sense of wonder ... to growing towards an understanding of fusion and our connections with all things on earth ... to the primary and instinctive need to take responsibility for a partner, and for the space around us. Pair-bonding is such an important part of our future development that surely the innocent exploration of our sexual boundaries should be recognised as perfectly acceptable. How else can we probe the mysteries of a meaningful union? Deep love and caring would ensure that one-night stands, which can never release the balanced energy we need for spiritual growth, do not become a major part of anyone's life. However, within the confines of real caring, making love with a number of partners may contribute to the knowledge and experience needed for a successful bonding.

A deeper pairing could be one in which additional commitments are made to raise a family. This is without doubt *the* most difficult and *the* most important job that any of us will tackle on the earth ... and it's the one for which we are least prepared. The increased responsibilities and inevitable sacrifices mean that very different criteria apply to the partnership. There is, of course, the basic need for deep love, care and concern, but in addition, each parent must want to sustain these, expanding them to include the children over a long period. The needs of such a partnership are very specific, and are of paramount importance in the nurturing of a family. Parenthood manifestly has its abundant blessings and rewards, but in the light of the importance of our individual journeys and development through our lives, the experiences may not necessarily provide a means of continued spiritual evolution for both partners after the children have grown up sufficiently to follow their own paths.

Another relationship may be one which stems from the acquired knowledge of the first two. There is a powerful subconscious desire in most people to reach a real understanding of our place in the universe, and the pairing for this infinitely rewarding search may not be the same as that for bringing up a family.

Yet another may be a period where you get to know yourself a little better by living alone for a while, learning to cope independently and grow personally through contact with friends and engagement with the local community. I had such a period for five years and learned an awful lot which I probably wouldn't have with a partner. At least I can iron my own shirts.

My present bonding with my partner, Ba Russell, has made this the most fulfilling, rewarding period in my life and has led to spiritual, mental and emotional growth beyond my dreams.

Religious and social pressures against the development of new relationships are subtle and powerful. It requires a great deal of personal courage to root out the deep-seated fears which guide most of us in our decision-making. Fear of hurting, fear of being alone, fear of an unknown future, fear of making a mistake, guilt from establishment codes of behaviour ... all of these make us hesitate. The decision may cause temporary pain and anguish but the trauma itself serves to heighten the potential for spiritual growth in all parties concerned, and the rewards are infinite.

My impression is that the beings at the end of the tunnel ... affectionately known to us now as The Management ... are looking forward positively to a change in the nature of human pair-bonding. They seem to prefer a more open, trusting and fulfilling association, with partners having their own equal and separate identities. Each can develop in their own way, unafraid, feeding the other with ideas, and having the time to discuss new thoughts and perceptions. Either one, if they find themselves moving ahead, will stop, reach down and yank their partner up beside them, keeping the balance of growth, like two columns supporting a common capstone. This visual symbol dates from Sumerian times, when the approach to social and religious problems was gentler and more balanced than our present crisis-to-crisis management. Partners will find that they work together more and more intuitively, and discover more subtle ways of communicating.

They will create and emanate an energy which stimulates and inspires everyone round them.

Energy of this nature is all-pervading. It arouses enthusiasm where there was lethargy. It excites people to question whether they can travel on a more rewarding path. It persuades those who have had only superficial relationships, which have no such energy, to dig deeper to find out what they are missing. It is one of the building blocks of a new society.

We were recently visited by a man who had been involved for the previous six months in the activities of the group who are protesting about the proliferation of motorways and aircraft runways in this country. The establishment-led media portrayal of scruffy but peaceful protesters who don't understand commercial pressures is belied by the existence of an astonishing core of disciplined, capable and talented people who have the future of our earth very much at heart.

In some ways they have gone back to the basics of community living to establish the group. Nothing really happens until the man of the fire decides where to light it and gets it going. The fireplace then becomes the power centre where everything happens. Cooking, discussion, organisation, eating, relaxation and planning take place around the flames which are never allowed to go out while the project is on. Different people have responsibilities for food supply, waste disposal, communications and the practical business of tunnelling and building, and liaisons grow between people not, as is often the case in our larger society, from loneliness, but from involvement in a common interest. They have developed powerful personal and community bonds in their commitment to this fundamental problem and have created an energy which cannot be denied. It has raised awareness in high places, and crucial decisions have to be made in the near future by our political masters concerning our environment and its management.

The group know, of course, that tunnelling and treehouse methods have probably had their day, since the authorities have learned how to deal with them, but it will be interesting to see how these dedicated people express their concern about environmental issues in the future. Apparently their relationship with the officials working to remove them was mainly cordial and good humoured and while many of the police expressed sympathy with their stance they had to carry out their job as instructed. There is no rancour between the two since the energy created by the various exercises has brought the transport and fossil fuel problem firmly into the public domain through television and will no doubt lead to a reappraisal of future development.

There are delicate forces at work to move us out of an apathy which was for a time in danger of convincing us that we can't alter things for the better.

Changes can stem from a personal level, with a simple but subtle shift of emphasis in our bonding.

Chapter Six

RELIGION THROUGH THE MYTHS OF TIME

EVEN A CASUAL look into man's stormy history reveals a great need for some form of stable focus around which a society can grow and develop its stories and legends. Something which gives a feeling of familiarity, of belonging, but with enough mystery to keep the ultimate understanding of it just out of reach. It has to be there all the time, reliable, without the confusion of change, and be easily accessible to everyone perhaps through a simple series of rituals or ceremonies.

Most religions, worldwide, have developed from this need. Man has always had a deep-seated feeling that, beyond his normal senses, he was part of something important which he didn't quite understand. It is firmly implanted in our subconscious and residual memory. The old people were well aware of energy and life-forces beyond our physical understanding, and endowed the planets and stars with qualities which they knew to be out there somewhere. There was a natural appreciation of the life-giving warmth and energy of the sun, an acknowledgment of the natural rhythms of the moon, an understanding of the energies which led to the development of the life-force. They knew they were not isolated from the cosmos. They were a part of creation and consequently connected to the divine. Because of their closeness to the earth, they were aware of the subtle influences of distant stars and planets on her energy field. They could feel the resulting nuances of changes in the geomagnetic fields around them which triggered messages to their physical bodies. Their religion was a natural one which was easily understandable by all. It was an acceptance that they were part of, and had a contribution to make to, the ultimate creator. They simply established their direct communication and worked with the natural cycles and rhythms of the universe.

It was perfectly rational to treat the Sun as a source of life, with the Moon, planets and stars following in varying orders of importance in the scheme of things. Hurricanes, thunder, lightning and the occasional rainbow were accepted as local manifestations of one of the aspects of the creator and were treated with respect and understanding. However, when the sun occasionally disappeared, or had odd lumps bitten out of it, there was some concern, perhaps even fear, that it might be an indication of changes to come in the future. A number of astute observers who had studied these strange effects took advantage of their knowledge to reassure everyone that they would come to no harm, and that everything was fine. These entrepreneurs increased their credibility no end by learning to prophesy when the next manifestations would occur and this put them in a position of considerable standing in the community. Gradually they were able to introduce some simple rituals to the procedures which helped them to establish a comfortably high place in the pecking order.

It wasn't long before the ritual became a necessary part of the process of contacting the Life Source, and slowly but inexorably the peoples' natural ability to be in direct touch with the creator was eroded. Ritualistic ceremonials were put in place by a growing hierarchy of intermediaries, dressed in increasingly bizarre ceremonial robes to emphasise the gulf between them and their congregation. Mysterious rites were introduced, and simple, honest and uncomplicated people were made to believe that they were not qualified to communicate directly with their maker.

This cynical insinuation between people and their harmony with gods, earth, and the cosmos created the potential for a vast manipulative power source. As people were distanced from a quiet rapport with their creator, a sense of vulnerability led to fear. The intermediaries grabbed the opportunity to invent mythical, vengeful gods, whose potential wrath threatened the very existence of anyone who did not conform to the ceremonial rites.

All over the world the build-up of power over people grew and festered, with very little regard for the welfare and quality of life of the majority of the increasing population. Ritual became dogma, and the dogma itself became so important that it became justifiable to kill anyone who dared to disagree with it. The simple, natural, and highly spiritual concepts of the old people were swept aside. They were labelled as pagan. The literal meaning of pagan is 'country-dweller', and it was when earth became synonymous with an invented underworld that pagans became personae non gratae. Who can possibly deny that each one of us is totally dependent on the earth and its rich resources for our very existence? A caring appreciation of the our home planet, earth, with its generous, unstinting provision of everything we need, in no way precludes us from understanding the ultimate grace of the divine.

The intercession of advanced beings like Buddha, Jesus and Mohammed should have given us a chance to break through barriers that were causing misunderstandings throughout the western world. The concept of love, caring and concern for all the living things around us, and for the planet we live on, is common to Christians, Jews, Buddhists and Muslims alike and is the fundamental platform from which any kind of advancement for our species can be made.

It must be heart-breaking for these avatars to see how their words have been censored and changed to create even more divisions among the people they tried to help.

The appalling atrocities committed in the name of all the various religions are documented endlessly, pungent with the particular prejudices of each writer. Perhaps a positive step forward could be made by leaders of all denominations by taking a good hard look at some of the legends and myths which have been used to establish ground rules for their particular cult. It just cannot be beyond them to comprehend that we desperately need a global understanding of our place in the universe and a simplified religious belief that satisfies us all.

The word religion comes from the Latin 'religio' meaning reunity, so perhaps we could get on to some common ground together by reviving the ancient ways of direct communication with our creator.

In the light of in-depth research over recent decades into the historical facts behind religions, it is perfectly obvious that there are serious discrepancies which must be addressed. In the Middle Ages the mere expression of doubt as to the truth of even minor parts of the myth was enough to label the doubter as a heretic, and burning at the stake was a sufficiently barbaric threat to keep all but the most dedicated very quiet.

The deeply religious and very advanced Albigenses paid a terrible price in the 12th century when Pope and French king combined to have them destroyed. They were branded as heretics simply because they did not accept one of the tenets of the Roman religion. The truth is perhaps that their life style was so rewarding, and their influence so great, that they became a threat to the political stability of the area and to the rigidity of control from Rome. Fifteen thousand people were butchered with the blessing of the Pope in the name of preserving Catholic dogma.

Our plundering Crusaders wreaked barbaric havoc over huge tracts of Europe and the Middle East shouting "for England and St George" as they maimed and murdered thousands of men, women and children whose beliefs didn't coincide with theirs.

Small wonder there was a tendency by ordinary people throughout the Western world not to upset the applecart by questioning what the local vicar said.

We are no longer in the Middle Ages and our emancipation and educational systems over the years are teaching us to think for ourselves. Perhaps we should all look for a clearer understanding of the original messages based on love and caring behind the various religions before they were downgraded and fragmented by people who saw them as a potential power source.

What could be simpler?

One of my first memories of a Presbyterian Church service was of the minister thumping the edge of his pulpit in the fervour of getting his message over. I was about six years old as he leaned over, fixing me with a gimlet eye, and bellowed loudly...

"I'll put the Fear of God in you!"

I remember feeling a bit confused because firstly, I'd just sung a hymn about how my God loved me, and secondly because, while I was being told what a mortal sinner I was, I could hear my friends outside playing football, yelling and thoroughly enjoying themselves. Apparently they had no idea they were sinners, and seemed none the worse for it. So naturally I joined them playing football the next week.

I have memories, around that time, as we streamed out of our grey Victorian school building at four o'clock, of the cry that arose with excitement every couple of weeks or so...

"Let's go an' thump the papes!"

Everyone would join in, including me, rushing in a crowd towards the school at the other end of the street. If they had a smaller mob than ours, we would have a joyous victory in chasing them down the road, and conversely, if there were more of them, we would beat a jeering but hasty retreat to return another day.

I quite seriously did not have the slightest idea why we performed this strange ritual. It was kind of fun unless you got involved too closely in the front end of the fracas, and it all happened because, for some reason, the inmates of the other school were different from us.

It was years later when I realised that they were, of course, Roman Catholics. The powerful forces which separate us on this earth because of our religious beliefs are sometimes introduced to the very young in strange innocent ways.

We have the sad situation now of Jews against Jews, Arabs warring with Arabs, Christians killing Christians, and all of them fighting each other in deep distrust of everyone else, mainly because of misinterpretations of ancient legend, some of them quite deliberate.

SIMPLICATE AND ADD LIGHTNESS

A number of widely experienced, longstanding members of the church, in various countries, agree in private conversation that they have to live with beliefs which are based largely on myth, but despair of being able to change the status quo without being ostracised from their community. It seems a pity that religious bodies tend to sustain traditions which were viable two thousand years ago, in the hope that people will continue to support them today. The fear that there might not be an alternative which will perpetuate the existing power structure seems to be one of the main reasons for resistance to change.

Truly enlightened people already have in their hearts and hands the solution to the great resurgence of spiritual yearning in many minds today. They are heading back to the basic teachings of all the world's great religious leaders, and moving firmly beyond the parochial squabblings of the various factions.

The Management has an overview on matters of religion which recognises our local earthly protective preoccupation with the legends and myths which have developed over generations. The differences in our beliefs create schisms important enough to fight over during our lifetime on earth, but they don't seem to have any relevance in the scheme of things in the angelic realm. All of our experiences in our human form, help to guide us towards spiritual growth, and they are interested in the level we've reached, rather than the extraordinary contortions we go through on our journey.

They are really concerned at the trauma, anguish and despair which we seem determined to create for ourselves while we are living in our density, and they reckon if we spent a fraction of the energy we dissipate on futile tribal posturing, we could evolve into a stronger, wiser, gentler species with the ability to connect directly with the higher beings in the universe.

Issoudun Sculptures

They have indicated quite clearly that we have the capacity to do it. We have a unique capability to live in the physical body, restricted to our five senses, and yet be aware of the supreme importance of our spiritual being.

WINDS OF CHANGE

It's encouraging, though, to see that there are signs of a change in our attitude to religion. In the inner cities, dedicated people work under the most stressful conditions with differing ethnic cultures, poverty, and deprivation, to show that the basis of spiritual growth is the same in any language. Thousands of well-informed people are looking for a simple form of faith less hidebound by archaic restriction. Russian Churches in the currently chaotic new political Republics, provide, with three choirs, candlelight and colour, a pure ethereal uplift, the language and words unimportant in the numinous extrasensory experience. Evolved men and women of all denominations work selflessly the world over, giving encouragement and help to anyone who needs it, regardless of their faith. Wherever there may be disaster through political and military aggression, hundreds of people of all nationalities appear from nowhere, often at great personal risk, to give active aid in any way they can. They are moved by compassion, their efforts are mostly unpaid and unsung, and their contribution lifts the human spirit.

At Issoudun, south of Vierzon in the Val de Loire, the local church has retained its old facade, but the interior has been refurbished to an exciting new concept, with lights, colour, superb gentle sculptures, paintings and stained glass which reflect the joy of enlightenment, rather than the implication that we must all suffer endless woe in order to move to the next level. At Taize, near Cluny in France, hordes of young pilgrims congregate to feel the joy of togetherness, chanting a recognition of their changing spiritual needs. In Liverpool, an interdenominational church holds services for all religions, inviting everyone to broaden their minds and accept the validity of legends other than their own. St James Church in Piccadilly runs services, lectures and seminars with an agenda so broad as to be unimaginable even a few years ago.

I have met and chatted rewardingly to many dog-collared gentlemen using dowsing rods. Among them are some delightfully advanced thinkers who do not seem to be in the least averse to confirming that the energy they are finding in the earth has a connection through the cosmos to the divine.

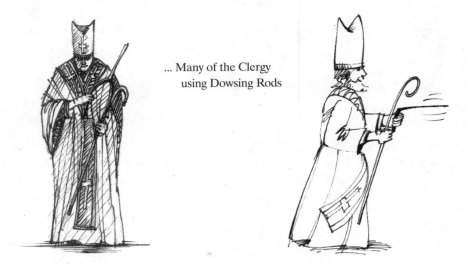

... Many of the Clergy
using Dowsing Rods

Perhaps we can move towards a time when religion is not an hour's performance in a ritual ceremony once or twice a month, but an altered way of living in which all decisions are made with primary regard as to how they affect people and our home planet.

It will require an earth-shaking paradigm shift of ten on the Richter scale to get to some of our business and political friends, who are making major decisions at the moment, but the angelic forces have a remarkable and heart-warming confidence, based on the current shifts in awareness, that this is going to happen in the near future.

Chapter Seven

THE BUSINESS OF MONEY

WEEKS OF DRY weather and temperatures in the mid-eighties had changed the mountain trail from a slippery sea of mud that needed a four-wheel drive vehicle, to an acrid, dusty red-orange, precipitous, but negotiable track. Our highly-polished compact Chev hired car wondered where on earth it was going as it crawled up the mountains behind Carmel. Great eagles wheeled with confident elegance in the crystal-clear air, and the sight of a group of vultures feeding on a carcass at the side of the track brought us in close contact with this untamed landscape.

We were heading for Ventana Wilderness Ranch, the ancestral home of the Esselen, the 'lost tribe' of California. They were the earliest inhabitants of the Big Sur Coast and, as native American people, had a deep reverence for the spirit of their land. Terry and Paige, our mentors and guides during our journey in America, had by some magical means contacted Tom Little Bear Nason, the spiritual leader of the tribe, and he had agreed to talk to us.

The temperature was in the nineties when Little Bear, a gentle giant, greeted us on arrival and led us to his traditional roundhouse. Its four massive timber columns supported the pole roof, and a ray of sunlight through the smoke hole

Dowsing Little Bear's Aura.

PAIGE CROWLEY

lit a four foot dreamcatcher suspended at the centre over the fireplace. The cool interior was below ground level, two-tier seating, dug from the clay, forming the circular walls.

He talked softly to us for a while, and after the simple cleansing ceremony of smudging with local wild sage and brushing us with black feathers, he introduced us to the spirit of his ancestors. Through the talking stick we explained why we wanted to see him, sharing our concerns about the earth and the ways of people living on it. With quiet dignity he told us stories of the native American people, without rancour or blame, and in the end we were in tears of shame. He illustrated his words by drawing in the dust with the end of the talking stick.

One of the most moving legends was of the four pairs of people, two red, two brown, two yellow, and two white, who met at the centre of the world. They each had a drum, and agreed to go in pairs in the four directions of the earth, to discover and experience its mysteries. When they had learned all they could, they would return to the centre to share their new knowledge.

The yellows went to the east and were given the blessing of great spiritual learning ... the browns travelled south, and found the joy of emotional involvement ... the reds went west and learned to live with the earth, taking from it only what was necessary for living ... the whites went to the north, stayed a while, and started to think and think.

They turned the drums sideways and made wheels; they built vehicles which kept them separate from the earth; they built high square houses so that they lived further and further from the earth; they thought and thought and developed ways of talking to each other without meeting ... and forgot that they had to return to the centre to share their new knowledge with everyone else.

The legends from Little Bear are an illustration of the shift from values which retain some depth of understanding of the meaning of our lives here, to the tortuous machinations of the business and financial world of today.

Money developed as a system of using tokens to alleviate the timing problems associated with the barter system. If you had an old goat and two rounds of ripe cheese and decided to trade them in for a kayak, you had to wait till you found someone who wanted both cheese and goat and also happened to have a spare canoe. Not easy in Milton Keynes. So lumps of iron, shells and all manner of things became the symbols of exchange value depending on what part of the world you were in. It seemed a neat solution and worked well until some bright sparks started hoarding them, messing up the system, and claiming that the tokens themselves were valuable rather than the energy released when they were exchanged. Dedicated token collectors began to forget why they were on the earth and over the years have created a situation in which money and business are taking over from politics and religion as manipulative power-sources.

Over the last hundred years the desire to make money has become the ritual pinnacle to which a vast number of people dedicate their lives. Replacing the reverence for our earth and our relationships with neighbours and friends, it seems that there is now only respect for the guile that gives the edge in a deal. This can be with second-hand cars, or in the mergers of monolithic companies. The same sort of people are involved, one lot with a smooth polished veneer, the others blatantly savage and uncaring in their dealings. The latter, of course, are the ones who arrange mergers.

Time was when business and financial people had a reasonable code of ethics. There were a few who didn't subscribe to it, but on the whole there was an understanding that grew from the old ways of dealing. Even in my time I remember going to weekly markets in Scotland, where everyone bought and sold their chickens, sheep, eggs, pigs and cattle, making bargains and deals all day on a handshake. At 5 o'clock in the afternoon everyone paid up and retired to chat, mulling over the day without the stress of wondering whether they were going to get their money. It was a simple unwritten law that if you didn't honour your handshake, you weren't allowed back in the market.

Perhaps the depravities revealed after the Second World War had an influence on the current lack of morality in business and finance. One large American arms manufacturing company which had astutely arranged to have its factories situated in both Germany and England, supplying both sides with gay abandon, actually sued their Government some time after the war had finished for bombing their German factories, and won the legal case for massive compensation! One of the great contributors to the loss of credibility in large conglomerates, banks and finance houses, was Weinstock, who was brought in by GEC in the early fifties to deal with their financial problems. His closures and sackings are a matter of public record, but his action in changing the goalposts in terms of honouring a recognised business obligation to pay accounts in thirty days had fundamental and far-reaching effects which still reverberate round the world. He arranged that the company would take ninety days' credit on payments to suppliers. Within a short time GEC were sitting on a positively embarrassing cash surplus, and the financial papers were speculating on how he was going to use it. A number of major companies, of course, followed suit, and actually began to delay payments even further. Heseltine, to his eternal shame, endorsed this gross survival tactic for businesses during the recent recession. Small companies and suppliers, who were still trying to retain some semblance of dignity and fair play, were forced to turn to the banks for support. As banks became more aware of the risks, they began to advise perfectly successful and well-managed small businesses, which had been hit by this major alteration in ethics, that they had been 'overtrading'. The jargonese was a little different then ... the term 'cash flow' became the in-word much later.

Since that time there has been a steady deterioration in business and financial morality. Banks have gradually alienated themselves from smaller private and business customers. Witness the condescension when one asks for a facility of three hundred pounds, compared with the almost magical production of the bottle of sherry, if the figure is nearer three hundred thousand. Local branch staff are at the tough end of a business where they are no longer allowed to use their discretion, hide-bound by directives coming from accountant-led computer programs, which, by their nature, cannot include integrity, honesty and ingenuity as a factor in their 'bottom line' accounting.

The financial world has a thin veneer of importance because of our current obsessions, but has lost its way completely in terms of rational human behaviour. There are a few who still retain some integrity and dignity, but so very many who seem to have no values other than those they can buy. Witness the groups of politicians and socialites who attended Maxwell's vulgar birthday extravaganzas, and their friends in the legal brotherhood who closed ranks to say there was 'not sufficient evidence' to prove that thousands of pensioners lost their savings to one of the most arrogant crooks in the business.

Our legal system has developed into a massively complicated web, and is in danger of total self-strangulation. It is no longer about a search for the truth, but fences endlessly with obscure points of law which have little relevance to reality. Naturally the untangling of this fearsome, man-made mesh allows the perpetrators to charge brobdignagian fees for untying one or two of the knots.

The 'very respectable' Barings Bank was destroyed by a chap gambling with its clients' money. 'Futures' stripped of the rolled umbrella, briefcase, and bowler hat, and all the claptrap that the establishment have created round it, is really about betting on the figures appearing on a computer screen at a certain time. These figures in turn are produced by a different lot of computers, and have no reference to anything other than an artificial souffle created by their own network.

Exactly the same result could have been achieved, perhaps with a lot more style, if young Leeson had walked out of the bank with all its funds, and put the lot on the 3.30 at Lingfield.

The posturings of some of the Lloyd's Names, who for years had been receiving an extremely good return on capital with which they did not actually have to part, was a sad reflection on how some people in the financial market-place no longer behave with any semblance of honour. They had embarked on a high-risk venture, and benefited from excellent payouts from a highly profitable business. When the chips are down, as for all of us, surely they have to shoulder the responsibility for their own decisions.

Too often we see groups of raddled computer clerks leaving their monitor screens to celebrate the 'success' of hawking after a particular currency. A drink in one hand, they clutch their cellular phones with the other in case something important happens between gulps. Their day's work has enabled a privileged few to make a great deal of money, and if this is at the expense of tens of thousands of reasonable, caring people, it does not come into their calculations. An emptier, more parasitic life-style would be quite difficult to invent.

The use of political influences in the business world has reached stages of immorality to which even the long-suffering British public are beginning to object. It is difficult to believe that someone of the calibre of Mark Thatcher could have made serious money in arms deals if he had not been privy to some pretty special information ... and did Mellors really ask us to believe that his function as 'door opener' to armaments sales had nothing to do with his position in government? Spare us, please, any more of the gobbledegook.

The list of antisocial, uncaring people in high places is disturbing and it is right that many of us are taking a long hard look at institutions, banks, business and politics with a clearer understanding of just how we are being manipulated.

... a more parasitic life-style would be difficult to invent.

THOUGHTS FOR THE FUTURE

To be sure the cut and thrust of business and finance is to some extent a test of endurance, nerves, determination and tenacity and, in order to survive, some difficult decisions have to be made. Talented people in all areas should be rewarded for their ability, and there is absolutely nothing wrong in success leading to a good financial return. There is a serious responsibility, however, on the shoulders of those who are, through hard work or circumstance, more fortunate than others.

They have a moral obligation to have compassion for those less blessed. Perhaps their consciences might be pricked if their actions and decisions have been made without consideration of the harm they may be doing to other people. In their position of power surely they must shoulder the responsibility for looking into their products to be certain that the resources of our planet are not being misused? If a major part of the British export drive depends on the production of more and more mechanisms to blow innocent men, women and children into bloody pieces, then perhaps we should sit down now and have a fundamental rethink on what successful export figures really mean. The argument that, if we don't make missiles and mines, someone else will, does not begin to hold water, and someone has to have the courage to put the case to the rest of humanity.

We have, through our own inaction, recently allowed our society to be manipulated by a series of self-centred entrepreneurs. One of these is Murdoch, who, through his personal empire of newspapers and television, is now capable of deciding which colour of government we will have here in Britain. He has found a format for selling newspapers which perpetuates the lowest forms of human endeavour. He uses these to provide vicarious titillation to a large number of people who are trapped in the boredom of a society where there's nothing more important than money. His cynical funding of sports, so that he can make people pay to see them through his satellite system, is destroying the clean, healthy image of the games, and is producing overpaid prima donnas who are no longer sportsmen. His manipulations to control digital television programmes will make it possible for him to have a huge influence on who or what we will be allowed to see on our screens.

Can we really blame him? Not a bit ... we are the ones who buy his newspapers in great numbers ... some of us, that is. Perhaps when a few thousand people begin to embrace a wider vision and move just a little way beyond the mind-numbing banality of the content of the papers, circulations will drop, the power-source will dim, and we will save a great number of trees from a terrible fate. Even now it has been admitted that sales figures are slipping and the tabloids are having to print more and more outrageous rubbish in a desperate attempt to survive. Hopefully the ubiquitous grip of television will also be loosened when hundreds of boring choices are available, and the self-destruct of drearily predictable programmes will be automatic. We might even get a better percentage of interesting viewing and a decent newspaper for general circulation.

Control through media has unfortunately become a fine art. It can be the subtle put-down of an otherwise popular figure by selecting and printing an unflattering photograph ... nobody is perfect all the time. Or it can be in hugely expensive marketing operations set up to promote political parties. Grinning and embarrassed party officials stand by mega-posters more suited to selling soap than political agenda. Everyone knows that advertisers deal in fable, stirring up feelings of envy, guilt and inadequacy in order to persuade people to buy or subscribe to things they don't really want. Perhaps there'll come a time when our politicians cotton on to the fact that straightforward honesty would be singularly more effective.

Fortunately, recognition of the nature of control systems is beginning to make them less effective.

Statistics are very often used out of context to create selling headlines, but a deeper look into them will reveal, perhaps surprisingly, that the world and its human population are not in quite so bad a shape as appears from the continuous media bombardment. We have huge problems in the logistics of looking after everyone properly, but these are made infinitely worse by the ambitions of a relative few who are blindly devoted to grabbing all they can in this lifetime. Amongst them are practical, intelligent people whose organisational talents are of the best. What a difference it would make if just a wee bit of spiritual awareness was introduced to their thought processes. It can be done and at the end of their term on earth the Management might excuse the useless pile of tokens they had made for themselves if they had accomplished something really worthwhile towards improving our quality of life.

There is, however, a distinct impression stirring that quite a number of advanced humans in positions of power have already made the transition. It takes immense courage and vision to carry out the sort of changes that Gorbachev, De Klerk and Mandela initiated, with the full realisation of the unpleasant personal consequences which would inevitably result. History will confirm the huge contribution these and similar men have made to the advancement of our species.

The main shift, however, will come from a basic desire in the hearts of most people to see a degree of fair play in their lifestyle. Thousands of employers really do care for their staff. The great majority of people work conscientiously and make themselves good at their job. They aim for high standards in everything they do and expect no less from those who employ them or see fit to lead them politically. It's because they care and are relatively honest that most of the institutions can continue to exist. It's a sad fact that many of the complexities in our society have developed because most of us are to a certain degree dishonest.

Consider the enormous amounts of time, energy, and futile effort that would be saved if we were all a little more truthful. If we were one hundred percent honest there would be no use for banks, police, law courts, locks, keys, security, most insurances, these dreadful car alarms which seem to work only at four o'clock in the morning, and a plethora of related activities.

Too much to hope for? Then let's put the power of thought into moving our standards of honesty just a few points up from where they are now. The results will be so rewarding that the upward curve of truth will be self-perpetuating.

This is in no way idealistic jingoism.

Senior physicists, dealing with ultimate concepts of the way the universe works, are now building in human thought as a major contributory factor in the equations which govern the cosmos.

Chapter Eight

TAKING CARE
OF YOUR VEHICLE

THERE IS NO doubt that the Management believe we are quite an important species. Even in our dense life form, where we have developed the five basic senses necessary for survival on this particular planet, we are incredibly adaptable. True, we can take only minimal alterations of temperature, gravitational pressure or air composition without artificial help, but within these boundaries we can quickly accommodate some pretty fundamental changes. They bend over backwards to take care of us, see us through our many stages of transition and, if we only knew it, are available at all times to assist us. What they cannot do, however, without being asked, is to interfere with things that may go wrong with our bodies, or with the many sources of stress imposed by current social mores, and our consequent aggressive and uncaring behaviour. Throughout our history misguided zealots, for no reason other than their private beliefs or an insane lust for power, have been prepared to inflict appalling traumatic experiences on people. The worst of these involved millions of people, but equally depraved in their own way are individuals prepared to impose mindless cruelties on immediate family, neighbours or innocent strangers.

The very existence of angelic beings is often called into question by people who can't believe that the horrors of war and genocide could be allowed to happen under their gentle guidance. The truth is they have to leave us to find our own solutions, so that we can continue to widen our perceptions, sometimes through bitter and cauterising experience. As more of us begin to realise that we have many lifetimes available to us to expand our understanding, this concept becomes less difficult to accept.

How often have we heard the cry...

"They should do something about it!"

It has such a familiar ring in terms of governments, police, the legal system and all authoritative bodies, but is actually the vocal expression of an unwillingness to accept our own accountability. Each and every one of us can evolve to a level where the concerted power of our minds could reduce the impact of aggressive behaviour, and guide us towards a more caring society

Sequoia Sempervirens

This is no idealistic dream.

I have a little Sequoia Sempervirens redwood tree in my sitting room. She's only fifteen inches high, very delicate, very feminine and a beautiful light green. She's being specially nurtured, and gets embarrassed when I chat to her and tell her that she's going to be a towering behemoth higher than a thirty-storey building, with a ecoclimate of her own in her top branches. She doesn't believe me yet, but somewhere deep down she knows, and is quietly determined to see if it can be done. It may take her a century or two, but given a good start she won't need me any more.

We all have a similar potential if we learn to use our minds in the right way.

Spiritual and mental health have a profound part to play in our evolution. That is not to say for a moment that we should neglect our physical bodies. On the contrary, a sound physique will allow us to live free from many of the burdens of pain and fragility that people suffer unnecessarily, and provide us with the extra energy we need to progress to higher states of awareness.

As the population of the world increases, we are going through a difficult time in the fight to preserve our health. Progress in medical technology has worked minor miracles in the treatment of disease. Some of the advances, however, include the use of very expensive equipment and medicines, and as our expectations grow for the availability of top-level treatment for everyone, it is not easy to see, in present circumstances, how the spiralling costs can be met. Embattled and exhausted doctors do as much as they can to combat the symptoms of our stressful and hedonistic lifestyles, and perhaps with a little thought we could help ourselves to alleviate many of the problems by looking after our own bodies with a bit more care.

If we decide to top up daily with large draughts of alcohol we have to take our own responsibility for a liver that will eventually look like an old leather boot, and if we persist in smoking we cannot in the end blame the Health Service for not being able to fix our carbon-encrusted plumbing so that we can breathe properly again. Convenience foods snatched in front of television not only provide an indigestible, synthetic diet, but create a whole new set of problems, not least by stopping family groups from sitting together for a while to share their experiences.

In fact perhaps we should have a serious look at the reasons behind much of our ill health. We are under considerable stress from conditions which did not exist in earlier, simpler times. Perhaps we have not yet really had time to adapt to the alteration of the speed of communication, from roughly six miles an hour on horseback to the 186,000 miles per second of our present systems.

Increased speeds of transport led to the need for synchronisation of clocks around the world. It all started because the railways had to get rid of roughly twenty-four minutes' time difference between sunset in London and sunset in Penzance, so that they could devise a workable timetable. On the surface it seemed a practical, progressive thing to do, but along with the development of a really accurate clock for exact longitudinal fixes during long voyages across the

... adapting to an altered speed of communication.

oceans, it led to our inevitable alienation from the natural cycles of the earth
and the universe. The complex communication and air transport network in our
developed society means that we can never go back to the rhythmic twenty-
eight-day period enjoyed by the plant, animal and mineral forms on our earth.
We should, however, recognise our artificially-contrived time cycles as a serious
contributory factor to the growing stresses in our lifestyle.

We have evolved over thousands of years, coping naturally with changing
earth and cosmic energies, but we are now reeling from the impact on our
subtle energy fields from man-made electromagnetic frequencies from radar,
telecommunications, cellular phone networks, radio, television, satellites,
overhead and underground electric cables, ultra-low-frequency communication
with nuclear submarines, and a plethora of unknown experimental stuff which
will no doubt come to light in the future.

It's no wonder our immune systems are breaking down under the strain.

Newly defined diseases such as Aids, ME, Motor Neurone, and Alzheimers
are manifesting, together with alarming increases in the incidence of pollution-
induced illnesses like asthma and skin cancer. It is perfectly obvious that it's
time we put the brakes on our headlong acceleration towards a scratch-card
society which requires instant results, without effort, and cares nothing for finer
values.

We are an adaptable species, but we need time to consolidate the changes
which have taken place, particularly over the last hundred years.

Can we relearn to use one of the simple systems our ancestors used to
considerable effect in staying healthy? Can we reawaken the ability to 'listen' to

our bodies? A generation has grown up with the belief that the only sources of nourishment available are in sanitised plastic packets on supermarket shelves. The marketing gurus, by some strange logic, have decided that the public do not want to be reminded that vegetables actually grow in the ground. So many of us now have to pay for the process of cleaning, scrubbing, and polishing our food to remove all traces of honest earth, spraying with preservative chemicals, and packaging to keep all the goodies looking pretty. All gardeners are aware of the enormous difference in the taste and goodness of their own vegetables compared with the processed stuff, just as cooks who still make their own soup find the taste of dry powdery packeted bits added to water pretty disgusting.

All right.

It takes a little more time.

But when we consider the tens of millions of hours wasted, as half the population wallow in the superficial wafflings of television soaps, perhaps a few minutes in preparing good, healthy, simple food might be well spent. Saves a fair amount of money, too, and that can't be bad.

With a little effort we can easily become sensitive to the internal responses from our body, which clearly indicate what is lacking in the system. It might start when you are aware of a little voice inside saying...

"I really don't fancy haggis again tonight."

Your metabolism is saying that it needs something else to balance itself.

If it goes on, a little more positively, to say...

"I'd quite like a steak and kidney pie, fresh broad beans and potatoes,"

you've got the message from your body that these three will do the trick. Vegetarians, of course, will be guided along their own path.

This is not *in any* way an invitation to self-indulgence. Nothing to do with stuffing yourself with chocolate when you get the urge. It's a reintroduction to an awareness of the subtle needs of your body ... a special rapport where you learn to listen to your very efficient internal guidance system, accept its messages, and react sensibly to them.

A little more good, healthy exercise wouldn't go amiss either. It became fashionable some years ago for schools to sell off their playing fields, which had suddenly become highly desirable sites on which to build more offices. Presumably the schools bought more computers for kids to crouch over. (I have nothing against computers if they are treated as our servants rather than our masters.) Luckily for the kids, statistics have already come up with quite alarming data on the serious threat to the future health of the growing generation when they are deprived of a good run about after a ball. Action is being taken, and more people are actually taking up sports and outdoor activities, making a conscious effort to feel fitter and better, rather than passively watching others do it. They are much happier for it, and generate the sort of energy needed to improve all of our lifestyles.

The introduction of management systems into our Health Service by a series of well-meaning but sadly inept civil servants has resulted in mountains of paper which effectively take up an awful lot of everyone's time This was predicted pretty accurately by all the people at the sharp end who actually work with patients. The paper was introduced to provide statistics on how efficient everyone is, yet anyone who has anything to do with hospitals and medical practice knows that the service is on the verge of breakdown. Politicians are quite sensitive about the Health Service, and they have developed natty ways of massaging the statistics to make sure they don't look too bad. So, if patients are discharged before they are really fit, to the dismay of the professionals attending them, it's politically O.K. because they will swell the treated case figures by getting a new hospital number when inevitably they have to come back.

And the honourable gentlemen can stand up in parliament and say, hand on heart, and with sonorous conviction...

"We have treated many more patients than the other lot did !"

They are a strange breed, really. There's usually a half-truth somewhere.

Hopefully someone with a modicum of organisational ability, who has the capacity to take a practical overview of the entire, immense problem, will turn up soon. Let's be prepared to reward this potential paragon handsomely. The Service is a gem well worth saving, and a competent hand at the wheel could save us all countless millions over the next few years.

Unfortunately free services of any kind tend to be abused and we can all contribute by taking more responsibility for our own fitness, rather than needlessly paralysing the whole organisation by insisting on treatment for minor malfunctions we can perfectly well deal with ourselves.

AN ALTERNATIVE MOVE FORWARD

One of the happier results triggered by the current difficulties is the growing appreciation of complementary and natural medical techniques. By no stretch of the imagination can they ever be a substitute for highly skilled practitioners at all levels in the medical professions, but they can make a very important contribution to the health of the nation in many ways.

Those who work in complementary medicine fields tend to have more time to spend with their patients and are therefore perhaps more aware of the stress and emotional factors which affect health. Their work, whatever technique is used, is usually based on relaxation, caring and listening, providing a service which is sadly lacking throughout our society today. With the best will in the world, doctors cannot any longer, under the current phase of relentless pressures of cash and time restrictions, provide this extra ingredient, which was an essential part of their work in years gone by. In fact recent reports show that they themselves are suffering more than most from stress-related illnesses.

A major part of the work carried out by the practitioners of alternative medicine is related to the reduction of stress. Meditation, in its purest form, is about finding a peaceful, quiet point within yourself, a space unique to you, where nothing and no one can intrude. It is a joyous and relaxing place, where your mind can expand without restriction. Whether it is done in a group with some guidance, or quietly with a partner, or by yourself, inside or out of doors, it is a powerful tool in the movement towards healthy spiritual and mental growth. Find a way that suits you, be at peace with it, and let it show you the gateways through your barrier fences. Once you have found it you can, with a little practice, take it around with you and use it, if you like, on top of a number thirty-nine to Charing Cross. There's no need to be po-faced about the method. It's there to induce relaxation, care and laughter and quite substantially increases the joy of living. We have recently been working with Sam Holland of Portland, Oregon, whose refreshing, good-humoured teaching of deep transitional meditation has taken us to some very rewarding levels of perception. His ongoing work on earth energy interpretation and healing takes him all over the globe and opens up new and exciting avenues of research. A wider and more advanced use of meditation could release huge amounts of money currently spent on pep pills and tranquillisers to deal with other much more urgent needs within the Health Service.

There are many new therapies and therapists for all sorts of conditions. They include aromatherapists, hypnotherapists, psychic and spiritual consultants, counselling therapists, homeopathic practitioners, reiki masters, sound therapists ... the list goes on. They all have a unique way of initiating the healing process and many of them are highly experienced experts in their field. The best results come from those who work quietly and simply, their reputations gradually building by word of mouth through their successful therapy. One of the main difficulties in selecting the right practitioner is forming a clear definition of your own needs. If you then shop around a bit, and listen, you will be drawn intuitively to the right person.

Some of them have developed ceremonies loosely adapted from old "B" movies in order to impress prospective clients. The truth is that the more theatrical the presentation, the less likely one is to benefit from the treatment.

There is no longer the slightest doubt that healing actually works. Established medical practitioners are still concerned at the antics of those on the fringe of the business and the success rates claimed by a few, but this reticence does not devalue the contribution that thousands of dedicated healers are making to the relief of dis-ease. Doctors and surgeons would be the last to claim that each and every member of the medical profession is a paragon of all the virtues. There is no easy way to define the parameters of healing work and any 'qualification' must come through the practical application of the process to produce results. Most competent healers are the first to recognise that success in their field comes from a combination of events from many levels, and their part may be just to be there and make connections. They are happy to be involved in the action, and it doesn't matter to them who claims the cure as long as it works.

We spend fortunes on the mechanical vehicles which carry our physical bodies about. We have them carefully serviced and tuned for long journeys. We say we cannot do without them, while knowing that they are destroying our environment. We are indulging, with this misuse of fossil fuels, in a global stupidity equivalent to burning our furniture, floors, doors, windows and finally roof joists, just in order to keep warm, then finding we have no home to live in. We may wake up, scared and wide-eyed before it is too late, but we still persist in using them as a symbol of success, turning a resolutely blind eye to the thousands of people who are killed and injured by them. We clean them, polish them, look after them, so that they will be preserved as long as possible, or give us a good return on our investment.

But do we seem to care as much for the infinitely more complex vehicle which carries our essence during our lifetime on earth? It is surely time to check on the kind of fuel and lubricants we use, to keep it serviced with all its parts in good working order, to see that we have brakes so that sometimes we can stop and think. It's taking us on long hard journeys, some much tougher than others, and if it is not working properly we can't swop it ... the one we've got is what we have to work with. Our continuing essence is its precious cargo and safe transport to higher realms its primary function.

Each one of us has a responsibility to give it every chance.

Chapter Nine

CALL IT NEW AGE
IF YOU LIKE

THERE WAS REALLY nothing New about the Age. It's a sort of umbrella heading that was, and is still, used by media to categorise practically anything that doesn't conform to the status quo. The re-examination of sacred cows has happened many times before, and is a necessary adjunct to our continuing evolution. If we do not continue to question established values and probe into their generic roots, we will have failed in one of our purposes on earth.

Strangely enough the current questioning of entrenched beliefs has a powerful ally in the new technologies of communication. Through a more discerning use of television, publishing, and the global network, people around the world are beginning to find audiences for their particular views. Eventually this may provide a forum for more informed and clearer understanding of geographical, national and social problems.

The corollary is that while it is relatively easy to attack and discredit established views, it is rather more difficult to substitute something better to replace them.

We are in an interesting in-between stage now, where increasing numbers of people, who are genuinely concerned at the way we are heading, are having the courage to express in no uncertain terms their doubts about the direction. As a result of this, while they are in a minority, they may have to cope with a feeling of alienation from a large part of society. It may make them feel slightly vulnerable. They are aware that something is wrong. They are aware that it is their responsibility to search out and do something about it . But they are not sure how to do it.

Our growing ability to tap into energies which trigger senses beyond the usual five is enabling us to break down our limiting perimeter fences. On the other side of these artificial boundaries the visions and concepts are of such purity and scale that, having touched them, we have to retreat within our shells to reappraise, and reassure ourselves that we can cope. For generations poets, painters and composers have agonised in their attempts to express some of the wonders beyond the veil. Some have managed to give us just an inkling, the thrust of their creations striking deep into our psyche.

We hear a lot of talk about 'new' vibrations reaching the earth in recent times, stimulating our latent senses, and allowing us to move to a higher level of awareness. I think it is much more likely that these frequencies have been in existence around the cosmos for aeons of time, and we are only now advancing to the state where we can react to them. There is a certain arrogance in our bland assumption that they are changing to suit us. Science has confirmed that the rate of the earth's rotation is decreasing very gradually. This, together with alterations in the energy output of the sun, coinciding occasionally with a proliferation of sunspots, induces small but important variations in the planet's magnetic fields. These in turn affect the biomagnetic fields of every living thing on earth, and such simple changes, along with a myriad of much more subtle cosmic influences, have a fundamental effect on our health and behaviour patterns. We are perfectly capable of adapting to these differing circumstances, and our recent research shows that there are simple but exciting ways in which all of us can take part in sharing a closer rapport with natural forces.

At the beginning of the journey to widen our perceptions, there is nothing wrong with hitching a lift occasionally, by tapping other people's experiences. The road seems full of pitfalls, and away in the distance are rapidly receding figures who have read all the books, and seem to know exactly where they are going. The feeling that you can't really start till you know a lot more through instruction, reading, or attending courses and lectures, is par for the course.

It is not a competition. Each of us has our own pace, and if what you are about to do doesn't feel right ... don't do it.

As soon as you open your mind, your intuition will begin to guide you. Someone might suggest going with them to hear a talk. Your eye may be caught by books and articles which would not have registered before. You'll gravitate to people who are searching, as you are, for a more rewarding life style. Perhaps you will become aware that you have been missing out on a richly satisfying part of your life.

At this stage, with information coming from all directions in a plethora of seminars and courses, you may become vulnerable to the blandishments of some of the fringe operators.

There is no justification whatsoever, in this new age, for the creation of pockets of elitists who claim to have special powers.

Whatever breakthroughs in understanding we have ... and it is encouraging to find increasing numbers of people who are prepared to question established boundaries of thought ... they pale into insignificance when we gain an insight, however slight, into the immensity of the creation of which we are a very small, but significant part.

For years now we have been involved in the aspirations, machinations, manipulations, stratagems and sometimes, alas, deceptions of some of the charlatans in the outer periphery of what is loosely described as the New Age. It is perhaps inevitable, but extremely unfortunate, that commercialism has devalued the search for a more graceful set of values. It is perfectly right and proper to expect a reasonable return for any of the therapies, the supply of cards and books, art, music, crystals, candles, incense, oils, clothes, jewellery and all the paraphernalia which goes with the search for wider truths. It is deplorable, however, to find a number of cynics who have used our temporary vulnerability and revitalised sense of wonder to make a quick buck.

We are not talking here of the thousands of people who are intrigued, stimulated, and genuinely involved in finding a gentler, more caring way to live. They are the salt of the earth and their time will come, probably much sooner than they think.

It's time we took up cudgels with the few who have latched on to this growing spiritual movement with a view to massaging either their ego or their bank account. In a world where so many people are searching, driven by a profound knowledge that all is not well, it is even more necessary that teachers, leaders, advisers and marketeers are seen to accept the responsibility for their advice, pronouncements, and products.

CHANNELLING

An increasing number of people claim the ability to channel, and there is no doubt that many are capable of contacting minds which no longer require a physical body to continue in existence. It is quite a problem, at first, to separate out the wheat from the chaff.

Some have personal subconscious needs which, apparently, can be expressed only through 'voices from the other side', Some indulge themselves in the mystique of communication in order to grab some attention which might otherwise be lacking. Another quite serious difficulty is that 'messages' are not necessarily couched in language, rather in nuance, and this can lead to considerable distortion and misinterpretation. Any revelations of any kind through these sources can assume a disproportionate importance if heard by an uncritical audience, and it is regrettable that an increasing number of people's lives have been considerably affected by the pronouncements of irresponsible channellers. Some of them 'innocently repeat what they get through', without regard for either the effect it will have on the listener, or whether the message has any validity. Many of the recipients can become deeply distressed about potential illnesses and dreadful happenings which have absolutely no part in their lives.

Some practitioners work on the client's ego, telling them that they are one of the chosen few who have special work to do. Presumably the victim has to go back for another series of readings to find out what the job is. Others imply that their listener has been chosen specially as one of 'The Nine' who, of course, will be the only ones privy to secret information from higher sources, and who will save the world when all of the rest of us are falling about. Another scenario is to be told that they are part of a group of twelve people, each identified with one of the saints, who have been drawn together, waiting for the mysterious thirteenth, who, they believe, will be Jesus, second time around. Some of these gullible cases then need help with normal living problems, and, as they are sincere and convinced in their new beliefs, it requires a lot of gentle probing to find out who planted the ideas. The common denominator is often a missing channeller who has now disappeared to another county ... or even country ... but who will appear again when The Time is Right to do individual and collective readings.

There are organisations who are preparing to build perfect temples, with minutely detailed dimensions and specifications on construction and materials, channelled, of course, from one of the Light Beings. All that is required to get the project (which, naturally, will raise the consciousness of all humanity) off the ground, is to send a contribution to a PO Box Number somewhere in America.

There is a proliferation of channelled books, many of which touch on one part or another of the instinctive old knowledge within us all, thereby ensuring a bit of credibility. If they tend to be repetitive, use quaint language, or come up with some really far-out ideas, the writer can avoid responsibility by claiming to be merely repeating what comes from the source. If they are created with sincerity to stimulate progressive thought, that's fine ... but if they are written to satisfy the ego of the channeller they are of marginal value.

Any channellers who claim to be under instruction from Lightmasters, Merlin, Sananda, Star Seedlings, or any of a plethora of funny names ... and who need you to hop on one leg four times widdershins round an obscure oak tree on an otherwise bare Welsh mountain in order to save the world from some terrible catastrophe, shouldn't really be taken seriously.

Yet there are just as ludicrous requirements from some sources.

A staggering number of people believe that a Spaceship Commander by the name of Ashtar, has been hanging about for nearly fifty years, waiting for the right time to snatch a special group of new elite from a disintegrating world. They're all going to get new bodies so that they can populate the earth with really nice people after the chaos, but woe betide them if they have any metal bits on them while they're beaming up and down. Bit tough on us blacksmiths. Decades of continuously postponed deadline dates for the Ascension have passed, but the sales of tapes and instructions for this and many other similar cults go on unabated. Perhaps the belief survives because it encompasses the exciting ingredient of space travel and makes use of the residual knowledge of our eventual ascension from dense to free life form.

•When we do ascend, each one of us will do it in our own way, through our own minds. It will take time and understanding, the process will be gentle and gradual, and there will be no Ashtar to make it an instant happening without any effort on our part.

Channelling has its own important input to the process. It is another way to work with senses beyond the normal five. In judging the importance of information received, there are some simple criteria to keep on the back burner.

In the first place one should not be too influenced by the source's choice of name. An 'Ascended Master' could quite easily be the equivalent of a celestial first year student doing some fun experiments with a new form of communication.

The angelic forces can convey clear messages of encouragement, love and guidance without the need of a name which implies evolved wisdom. In fact the grander the name the less likely a genuine master would be inclined to use it.

If the content of the message is a touch long winded, uses 'thee' and 'thou' a lot , says 'You've done very well' ... and particularly if it comes up with 'dear children', stand back and give it a good, long, hard look. The beings with something worthwhile to say can do so with elegant simplicity.

In assessing the value of any information which, however subtly, pressures us to conform to behaviour, ceremony, or actions with which we are not completely happy, we should all be guided by our own discernment and intuition. Common sense rules apply to the art of judging channelling as much as anything else. We have to look at the person, their motivation, sincerity and honesty, then decide whether their belief is genuine that our essence continues its cycle in a more advanced form after our time here on earth.

Channellers with the skill to interpret messages from a higher source feel a strong responsibility to spread their inspired knowledge. Those of the calibre of Julie Soskin and Ruth White have an aura of humility, strength, and integrity, stemming from their continual contact with outside sources, and their work is geared to open more of our minds to receive guidance from the Management. It will enable new concepts to impinge quietly on our higher consciousness, and help us towards a clearer understanding of the extraordinary path on which we are travelling.

CONS AND CONTRAPTIONS

On a more material level, many of the strange devices offered for sale deserve an accolade of some kind for sheer inventiveness. Apparently one needs weapons of starkly differing characteristics to combat Venusians, as against Martians, or Aliens from Deep Space. It is reassuring that, wherever the threat comes from in the universe, manufacturers are already at work producing suitable arms to ensure the swift vaporisation of the Invaders.

Less amusing is a disturbing tendency by some suppliers to induce an element of fear in the presentation of their product.

Not long ago a friend of mine was persuaded, in a moment of weakness, to buy a bizarre device purporting to be an Awareness Amplifier. It duly arrived, all of three hundred pounds' worth, with a complex-looking array of little buttons set deep under the sealed glass top of a sturdy, nicely-varnished wooden box. Green baize material on the base completed the luxury look.

It looked fine on the table, but the recipient was a little unhappy, after a while, about its practical function and rang the supplier for some advice.

"If it's not working properly it's probably the Time Shift that got out of synch during transit," came the voice.

"Shall I send it back for checking?"

"Not necessary,"... with peremptory authority ... "We can fix it over the phone but on no account break into the sealed box."

There was a veiled threat that something awful might happen should this be done. Fear of the unknown is a powerful one to cope with, and the device found its way to my workshop to be looked at and, if necessary, dealt with. The forge, with its simple alchemy of fire, air, earth and water, and its capacity for purification, is a wonderful place to carry out this sort of work. Some delicate surgery with a small Irish Persuader revealed the contents. It was a standard Casio calculator of the type available in any stationery shop for about ten pounds.

My friend is a sensitive, innocently searching for the right path, and in that sense vulnerable to the trickery of unscrupulous manufacturers. My first reaction was anger that she had been made the victim of this cynical piece of fraud. We pursued the supplier through a maze of changed names, defunct telephone numbers and Post Office returns of 'Not known at this address', until one day we had another look at the order form which had been enclosed with the package.

Our attention was drawn to an item called a 'Healer Resonator' offered for sale at a staggering two hundred thousand pounds. It occurred to us that if someone had actually bought one, it might explain the rapid disappearance of the company.

If anyone in the Cayman Islands chances to see a little man sitting on the beach, whittling thick bits of wood and carrying a bagful of Casio calculators, we would rather like to hear.

A bewildering array of gadgets is available to alleviate real and imaginary problems. There are lumps of plastic with imbedded whirlygigs of copper wire and little crystals ... silver mounted original slivers of wood straight from Golgotha (simple maths seems to indicate that the cross must have been a couple of hundred metres long) ... intricate presentations of feathers, bones and assorted natural bits in all shapes and sizes ... all of which claim to sort out everything from unstuck relationships to athlete's foot. Their redeeming feature is often that they can be quite decorative. Some, on the contrary, are dull, efficient-looking metal boxes with lots of impressive cable coming out from a carefully insulated hole, and deal with 'black streams' of energy. On inspection quite a number, regrettably, are found to have nothing inside them. Others have strange electrical parts and claim to create conditions of minimum geopathic stress and a safe place to sleep. The interactions of the earth's magnetic fields with our own biomagnetic fields are extremely complex, and this approach does not begin to address the problem. Much more about this in a later chapter.

Apart from some of these more outrageous products most of the bits and pieces are relatively harmless, and not too expensive. If people really believe that their acquisition will help them over a few hurdles on their journey, then perhaps the gimmick has served its purpose. If they are effective in helping to concentrate the mind on a particular problem it may be impossible to calculate their value.

We mustn't lose our sense of humour, either, and a recent advertisement for a wire pyramid, which read...

"Beat the Rush! Ascend Now !"

evoked a healthy chortle, and *almost* made me part with my money.

There has been a welcome reduction in advertising the more bizarre fringe trivia in the last year or so, as responsible publications began to get worried about the effect on their own credibility. It's not so easy now to find chakra trimmers, anti-grav necklaces, geopathic reversers and UFO listening devices with inbuilt translators, but I have no doubt that if you really need one someone will be happy to supply.

There are still a few courses that one should have a wee look at before committing...

"YOU too can be an AVATAR"
Weekend Workshop in Wimbledon Sat/Sun 10a.m.till 4 p.m.
Advance Bookings Only. £325. PO Box 666 Wimbledon
Bring food for sharing.

It pays to dig a little to find out exactly what the advertisers are offering. An Avatar is the most highly evolved being who can still exist within the human body.

Can you do it in a weekend?

In Wimbledon?

The rules, of course, also apply to more modest claims, and should always be applied before you write your cheque.

There are a number of discerning magazines dealing with New Age material. The searching, stimulating material in *Resurgence* has international appeal; *Caduceus* is slanted to health and healing matters; and a browse through *Kindred Spirit* with its intriguing articles and selective coverage of available therapies and courses can be a rewarding experience. One or two of the items may leap at you out of the page, and it is important that this instinctive rapport is recognised before the rational mind tries to take over. It's part of the natural guidance which will develop during the journey.

In most cases where we are striving to stretch our minds beyond the normal five senses, the use of electrical, mechanical and natural artefacts is quite simply to help us to concentrate. This is not to denigrate their purpose but to suggest that we are perhaps capable of achieving the same results through pure thought. The use of crystals is believed by some people to be necessary in certain methods of healing. There is no doubt that a ritual which includes them helps to focus the healer and makes the work easier. However it seems reasonable to suggest that we can develop the potential of our minds more positively without recourse to using props. Experiments have shown that if the crystals are replaced by pieces of paper on which their names have been written, the treatment can be just as effective. It would seem that the most important factor in all this kind of work is the 'intent' in the minds of everyone involved.

We are groping towards the one hundred per cent concentration that we need to accomplish all we want to do. In the right circumstances we can walk through a wall. All we have to do is hold our purpose with absolute clarity! The last one per cent or so is the real problem. Painful experiments, and a slightly bent nose, have confirmed that at least one of us has not yet reached the required level. There is still the little voice which seems to come in at the moment of contact saying...

"What if...?"

Walking through Walls
... Hold our purpose with absolute clarity!

If we are to cross new frontiers we have to do it through mind alone, and it will require some assiduous practice.

REGRESSION

Regression can be another source of guidance and misguidance. Organised by someone with experience and understanding, it is an interesting exercise. It's another way to open minds to concepts and possibilities beyond normal experience. Probing into previous lives, real or imagined, can be fascinating. We are learning that there's a bit more to life than three score years and ten, and the Management are encouraging us in many ways to break out from our self-imposed strictures. Trouble is that as soon as we find another way to go, we tend to assess it from our present rather gloomy standards. How often have we heard from a regressee...

"No wonder I'm in a mess—do you know what happened to me a couple of thousand years ago?"

A disconcerting number of them seem to have been well known historic figures. Lots of Cleopatras, Nefertities, and assorted high priestesses ... quite a few Merlins, Caesars, rampaging Knights and a miscellany of Holy Willies. Not many peasants, I'm afraid, although serious regressers have recorded fascinating, detailed lifetimes through many periods of extremely hard living conditions.

It is essential, whatever discipline we are following, to appreciate the absolute importance of *this moment in our lives*.

'Now' is the only reality.

Every lifetime, every experience, every relationship we've had, has strengthened each of us emotionally, physically and mentally, to make us what we are at this particular point in time. The past is always interesting. We can dwell in it with nostalgia. We can look to it to refresh our memories.

What we cannot do is change it.

We can prepare ourselves for future times. We can make as many plans as a Buff Orpington can lay eggs. We can organise, save, anticipate, speculate about happenings to come, and it is certainly a wise thing to do. We can choose certain paths to follow but we cannot, if we are willing to evolve freely, predict where the path will lead. We are on a great pilgrimage. There is excitement in anticipation of the unknown round the corner, and the challenge will sharpen our senses.

We should learn to be accountable for our own decisions, and be prepared to take the first steps *now*.

The most critical moment of our lives is this one.

Many are not moving forward because they insist that they still have 'stuff' to get rid of from past and present life times. It has them in stasis and provides the excuse not to go further because they are still controlled by fear. As soon as a commitment is made to start the journey, the 'stuff', having served its purpose, will be eliminated.

It takes a deal of courage, and waverers are open to pressures from many sources to conform to one discipline or the other.

Sai Baba   Mother Mira

GURUS

There are gurus for every persuasion. Followers of Sai Baba believe that he is the reincarnation of a very advanced being. His work in India is beyond reproach and he is capable of using energies to manifest things like watches, rings and Vibuti. People are drawn by his charisma and are prepared to sit for days in regimented rows just to see him. There is nothing wrong with that, and his presence satisfies the need in thousands of people to follow a leader. His disciples come from all nationalities and walks of life, and for many of them the journey and their time in the ashram provides a deep spiritual experience.

It remains for each of us to decide whether that particular path is one to follow.

Mother Mira in Germany is an enigmatic and highly evolved being. She works creatively with the energies, and in silence, using only her mind, contacts each separate person in her audience. Every one receives a different message. It can be a possible solution to a problem, quiet guidance on a path to follow, or a simple clarification of thoughts. Her presence is inspiring. At the end of the silent session she invites each one to come near and respond to her warmth. At that moment, if you are ready, she can, through her gentle eye contact, complete the circuits which will help you to communicate directly with the Management.

There are also fashionable gurus who, like fireworks, ascend briefly, make loud noises, and burst gloriously but momentarily on the scene before sinking without trace.

Others, less harmonious, collect vulnerable emotional cripples around them, impose arrogant, egotistical disciplines on their flock, usually demand droit de seigneur, and arrange for all financial deals to be handled through their own personal bank account. They are dotted around the world, and are the very antithesis of the developing spiritual movement.

There are always difficulties in moving established belief systems from one culture to another. A representative of the British Medical Council, with reference to Chinese medicine, once pronounced...

"If we could just get some of the main ingredients into a proper pill, it might be worthwhile giving it a trial."

Most of the deep knowledge of thousands of years of study and preparation would be ignored. Each one of us is unique, our requirements are different, and the traditional treatment by Chinese medical practitioners recognises our singular needs.

In similar vein, the subtleties behind the life-styles of generations of Tibetans become blurred when we try to transfer their meditative processes to our western culture. Their spiritual guidance came from the same generic base, but its development has been influenced by immensely different social and geographical criteria. Centuries of programming on opposite sides of the world have created the potential for problems when we meet to exchange ideas. We can learn a great deal from each other, but we must be prepared, if necessary, to change the goalposts. A sad illustration of the gulf that can exist between east and west was headlined recently in the legal action by an American woman against an eastern teacher who included Tantric sex in his therapy.

Occasionally we come across not a guru, but a gentle, thoughtful man of the calibre of Bede Griffiths, who worked latterly in India. He was able to cross cultures with compassion and understanding, and showed us that our time here can be spent in close communication with the angelic forces. There are many such beings, of both sexes, who work quietly and alone, without media or popular hype, and their work is no less important for its serenity.

GUIDES

Many of us on the quest are occasionally aware of presences who appear to be acting as guides. The Management are always available if they are asked, and there is strong support for the belief that, at times, they partially manifest themselves in forms which we find easy to accept.

My own experience of them has been incredibly rewarding, although our meetings have been few and far between. The angelic forces have an intimate knowledge of each one of us, and the guise they appear in seems to give us the opportunity to work with them, but still retain a strong element of freedom of choice.

Shortly after I had started dowsing, and was beginning to find out a little about earth energies, I became aware of a supportive presence each time I began to question the validity of the work. Two or three times the energy-form took the shape of a diminutive Chinese in native costume. He had very long finger nails, and spent most of his time lying on his back on the floor with his little legs kicking the air, helpless with laughter, while he mimicked my use of the dowsing rods with his thin hands.

My Chinese Guide in Action

It seemed a bit odd, but I realised later that the laughter was with me, rather than at me. Far from ridiculing the rods, he was indicating that I was taking my first stumbling steps towards something which could be quite important. I was never able to call him up, but knew that he would appear if it was absolutely necessary. I have the same feeling with my connection with the Management. They have an awful lot to do, and I feel that I should not disturb them unless I'm really stuck.

One evening my little Chinaman appeared in a slightly subdued state, and indicated that I should follow him. I walked, or rather floated, behind him along a series of darkish tunnels till, finally, he came to an entrance to what appeared to be a huge cavern. He stepped aside, smiled a little sadly, and beckoned me through. It was the last I saw of him, and I had a great sense of loss as I walked past him into a sort of gallery half way up the side of the cavern.

I could see down an immense distance below me, and away above, remote and inaccessible, on a towering, sculptured chair carved from the living granite, sat a magisterial figure in a voluminous green cloak. He was surrounded by light, and as I went in he turned slowly and looked down at me. His face was parchment colour, and the dark piercing eyes completed his startling likeness to a century-old version of Picasso.

I started to voice a question, but realised that he knew what I was going to ask before a sound came. He said nothing, but looked down at me as though I was beneath contempt. In that moment, of course, I was aware that I already knew the answer. I moved away, chastened by the knowledge that I should have recognised the solution within me, and concerned that I had intruded on something much more important. In all the time he guided me, he never ever spoke a word. Each time I went into his presence with an apparently insolvable problem, he turned and gave me the look, hammering home the message that I already had the answers inside me, if only I would take the time to search.

Finally, in different mode, I went to the cavern just to thank him for all he had taught, and to my surprise found myself walking in at the same level as his massive chair. He still said nothing, but indicated that I should sit for a moment beside him. He nodded in the direction of the distant space below him, and I began to discern the thousands of changing scenes of activity which he was quietly observing. Again without a word, he looked at me with a barely perceptible softening of his eyes. I began to understand the immensity of what he was doing, but with a gentle dismissive gesture of his head he indicated that I should move on, and climb up through the top of the cavern. I looked back, and was shamefully aware once more of the trifling nature of the problems which I had brought to him.

The next guides were a very different kettle of fish.

I reached the top to find that the roof seemed to be made from a thin but very tough crystalline sheet. There was no other way to go, and on looking around I found a neat round hole about the diameter of a decent-sized whisky glass. Squeezing through took forever, and I was intrigued to find myself in a warm, friendly, happy area, full of bursting invigorating energy. Gradually I realised that the compelling, infectious noise and laughter filling the place was coming from a gathering of exuberantly mobile spheres and ovoids of all sizes, each of them in a different soft pastel colour. I thought that surely there must be some sort of goddess in charge, who would be in a proper recognisable human form, so that I could communicate. No sooner had the thought formed than the nearest bubbles responded with rippling laughter, the sound travelling infectiously and almost instantaneously through the entire group. By now there must have been hundreds, all chattering and extremely interested in what was going on.

Although the laughter was difficult to resist, I gathered some dignity and asked what could be odd about my idea of wanting to talk to a human-like goddess. The chuckling voices came back...

"Have you seen yourself lately?"

I hadn't thought of that of course, and they obligingly arranged to move my essence out of my 'body' temporarily so that I could see what I looked like. I have to confess to being more than slightly disconcerted to find, instead of my familiar shape, something very reminiscent of a very tall, thin, stretched condom. The transformation was difficult to assimilate at first, but very quickly it became a great joy to be able to move around with no physical restriction, and have the infinite pleasure of working with these delightful beings. They seem to understand all language throughout all time, exchange information instantaneously, express a great interest in everyone and everything they come across, and are always cheerfully ready to assist in any work we do.

When dealing with oddities in the earth's field, or entities who need guidance, we sometimes get a bit out of our depth. We only have to ask them to give us a hand, and they arrive, chattering, to sort things out. They seem delighted that we refer to them affectionately as The Helpers.

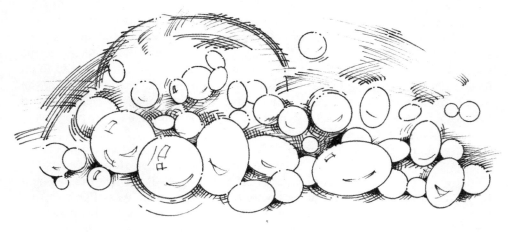

The Helpers

One of the most important things about guides is that nobody should feel deprived if they haven't got one. In fact most of us are unaware that they exist. There is nothing special about people who have guides. In fact those who have are sometimes prevented from making their own decisions by their apparent dependence on advice from higher sources. They are energy forms, manifested by the Management, which we can interpret at the extreme ranges of our five senses. Our sensitivities develop as we work with them, and the fact that they might not be recognisable as familiar life-forms doesn't matter a bit. We can benefit from their guidance but, as they are transient beings, we should be careful about trying to treat them as permanent fixtures.

Each One Unique

Time was when ostentatious behaviour was the In Thing amongst New Age participants. It was necessary in the beginning to shout loudly to be heard. At the early Festivals of Body Mind and Spirit long hair and sloppy sandals meant that you were really aware. There was a plethora of young mothers squatting in the middle of main crossings between the stalls, causing major pedestrian traffic problems, suckling their young with theatrical flashings of bare breasts ... smoke signals from a hundred spliffs billowing from behind counters, the distinctive aroma partially disguised by perfumed candles, incense burners, and aromatic oils ... tacky products, ill-presented, shaking in the reverberations from wailing loudspeakers spewing synthesised sounds ... and practitioners of questionable therapies looking po-faced and pure.

It is no longer so.

New Age is coming of age. The crowds at Festivals of Body, Mind, and Spirit are there to find out what is really going on. They are from a total cross-section of social and intellectual strata, wear the sort of clothes that people wear anywhere, and quite a number of the browsing hairy brigade seem to have a quiet PhD in Cybernetics, or something equally impressive tucked up their sleeves. People are disturbed and unhappy with current social and economic codes of practice, and they want to hear alternative ideas which may lead to an improvement in their lifestyle. The quality of the music, therapy, books, the wares for sale at the stalls, and particularly the content of the lectures and discussions, has improved beyond measure, and is a reflection of the progress to serious debate on the problems which affect us all.

The global initiative agreed by 178 nations at Rio in 1992, concerning sustainable development and the environment, was a huge step forward. The media treated it as a non- event but the effects, in spite of the fact that we hear very little about it, are spreading exponentially. Even in West Penwith, the almost isolated tip of Cornwall, a new appointment has recently been created for an experienced man to co-ordinate the efforts of the many separate groups who are working independently, many of them voluntarily, in a bid to improve the quality of our surroundings. This appointment was made possible by the agenda of the Rio meeting and is part of the move to create a vision for the twenty-first century.

There is still a minority of people who, while they hold ceremonies at sacred sites for the care of our Earth Mother, are blind to the need to clear up their twentieth-century rubbish after them. This is a measure of the lack of sensitivity prevalent in a small part of our society. In the same context, most travellers have a special relationship with nature, and are expressing their deep concern about present-day mores by jumping off the treadmill. Their image is tarnished by the few who destroy natural habitat with their detritus, and who unfortunately get all the media coverage. Caring and reasonably-behaved people in all walks of life are not news, and it is not surprising that we begin to believe that the constantly depressing TV and newspaper reports are a true representation of our society. If it were so, we would be in a pretty sorry state, and it would be difficult to be optimistic about our future.

However, encouragingly and perhaps surprisingly, most people do care quite a lot. We have to work on the few who, when asked to shoulder their own responsibility, lash out, kicking and screaming, blaming anyone but themselves for their situation.

A proportion of these are truly not capable of handling their lives. They may have been shattered by traumatic relationships, loss of family, or illness. For whatever reason, the stronger, more capable members of society must surely be prepared to help them.

Currently drugs-related problems are seriously contributing to the difficulties of developing a healthy and less aggressive society. While it is laudable for the authorities to nail a few couriers, yachtsmen and fishermen, with accompanying headlines shrieking the street value of the plastic wrapped catches, it is becoming less easy to believe that the businessmen who grow, manufacture and sell drugs keep their money under the mattress. The resulting lump would at least give them severe backache and make it dangerous for them to turn over in bed. At very high levels there must be a well organised 'Nelson' system of turning a blind eye by some banks and businesses to arrange the laundering of the enormous amounts of money generated world-wide. The monstrous immorality of such a set-up causes endless international distress. It not only degrades and destroys the health of drug users, but causes inexcusable grief to the thousands who are burgled, robbed and mugged by those whose addiction has to be satisfied, no matter what.

It is widely accepted that humans throughout their history have used natural drugs to stimulate their senses. Plants that grew in the countryside, like hemp, which not so long ago could be found growing wild in our modern hedgerows, provided a simple balance of medical and social needs. Strange brews, even worse than Japanese whisky, were concocted for festive occasions, and, because they were available only at special times, they probably did little harm. Nowadays the addiction to alcohol, nicotine and the harder drugs is having a profound effect on the living standards of everyone on earth.

Nicotine fills our hospital wards with people who, because of their habit, can no longer have an independent life. Alcohol, taken in excess, has an appalling record of creating altered states where any social conscience disappears, and aggressive and irresponsible behaviour becomes the norm. Statistics worldwide on those who are killed and injured on the roads by people who are under its influence would horrify a more caring society.

It's irrational to expect everyone to stop using all forms of drugs, since their use has been a part of tens of thousands of years of evolution. I am the first to confess that, after a day's work, a glass of whisky and soda goes down very well. (It's cooking whisky in case the aficionados of malts take offence.) It is more rational to try to move towards a society in which there is no longer the need for the *excessive* use of artificial stimulants.

This is where the thinking in this age of questing may help. Drugs are principally used to try and reach levels of existence which are not attainable in normal circumstances. A state of total relaxation, euphoria, or simple feel-good factor is the aim of most occasional users and I can see no cogent argument against that.

It is exactly the same goal as we have in our search for new values, but there are two or three major advantages in the way we are trying to do it. The first is that it doesn't cost us anything, and that helps to release the grip of the drug barons ... the second is that we don't have a 'downer' when the drug wears off ... and the third, and most important, is that when we reach these states we can react to them, appreciate them, and learn from them with all of our extended senses, without the distortions caused by the drug.

In order to develop a greater understanding of our potential, it is important for each one of us to know that we have a meaningful place in the cosmos. It's not an easy concept to take on board, considering the awesome size and age of the universe, but we have a parallel example in microcosm on our television screens. Every coloured picture is made up of thousands of little dots called pixels. Our eyes take in the masses of dots, not as individuals, but as a graphic illustration of what they mean as a group. Each pixel has its own individuality, having a special colour which contributes to the whole picture.

If one of these pixels suddenly decided that the effort to retain its own personality was no longer worth while, and it would be much easier just to be white, a little pinhole of nothing would appear somewhere on the screen. Other pixels might say...

"Why should I make the effort if that one's not going to bother?"

and, as this sort of behaviour is contagious, many more would soon drop out. The coloured picture would begin to lose its clarity, and eventually would become so blurred that the image would cease to have meaning. At that stage the rest would gradually give up, until only a blank white square was left.

Each one of us has a positive role to play in the cosmic game, and opting out is no help to anyone.

New Age thinking can provide the foundation and platform for individuals to start a new journey. The following chapters suggest one simple way to cross the threshold. Whichever way you go, the first step forward into the unknown has great significance. Even more important is the moment when the back foot follows in a gesture of commitment.

Chapter Ten

ONE WAY AHEAD

MANY PEOPLE ARE ready and eager to turn their backs on the 'rewards' from a boring material society and get going on a journey to redress the balance of their lives with an emphasis on deeper spiritual commitment. This has nothing to do with 'spiritualism' or 'religion' per se, but is the flux that connects us with everything, through all life on the earth, in the cosmos, and finally with the ultimate creator.

It seems such a simple thing to do.

It's just that when you are mentally, emotionally and physically prepared for the pilgrimage there is a whacking great gap in the knowledge of how to start.

There is a need for a positive, practical way of demonstrating that the extra senses which we have all suspected are there, really exist, and can lead to positive progress to a new understanding of our function in the universe.

One way, strangely enough, is through the art of dowsing.

The single, most important and unshakeable truth about dowsing is that everyone can do it.

There has been a paradigm shift in the acceptance of the process, illustrated perfectly by two dictionary definitions, one from a few years ago, and a recent one by a more informed compiler. The first is clear and uncompromising...

'Dowsing... The use of a divining rod or pendulum to find underground water or minerals.'

Full stop... Perhaps the sort of bald statement that means end of story for many people. There is, however, a wealth of difference in the implications behind the second interpretation.

'Dowsing... The use of *apparently paranormal* powers *to make discoveries* (my italics).

This moves the art of dowsing from a fairly humdrum but intriguing ability to an extraordinary talent which makes use of senses beyond our normal five. At a recent Congress of the British Society of Dowsers the resident scientist admitted that, although he was reluctant to accept that we were using a sixth sense, he agreed that we might well be using five and a half! In the old days of billiard-ball physics, dowsing didn't fit into a specific pigeon hole and, as it could not produce endlessly repeated results in laboratory conditions, was not considered to be a viable source of information.

Happily the present generation of physicists, through their study of the quantum theory, have become the new mystics, prepared to acknowledge forces and influences which had no recognised existence in Newton's time. During our visit to Russia in March 1991 we worked with professors of physics, geology and geophysics in Moscow, St Petersburg and Kiev on earth-energy projects and the effects of biomagnetic fields. Many of them were astonished to find that information from dowsing tools, which they used regularly in their work, was not found to be acceptable in other parts of the world. In his wonderfully researched book **The Dance of the Wu Li Masters** Gary Zukav expertly explores the complex world of quantum thinking, simplifying the language and probing deep into the expansive and uninhibited minds of the physicists. The strange unpredictable behaviour of matter at this level has released them from the previously restricting parameters of their academic discipline and led them, through their scientific findings, to some astonishing parallels with many of the principles of ancient Buddhist philosophy. Recent work on earth and cosmic energies using dowsing techniques seems to support some of the more advanced concepts proposed by these scientific frontiersmen.

Everyone has the ability to dowse to a greater or lesser extent.

It does help a great deal, however, if your mind is open. For most of our lives we are subject to imposed belief-systems through education, environment, religion, social status and a host of other controls which tend, as we grow older, to become more rigid. Some of us require a traumatic experience to shift us into a more receptive mode. It certainly happened to me, but fortunately most people don't need such a kick in the rear as I did, and are able to slip naturally into a wider understanding of the deeper meaning of the universe.

Dowsing is a fascinating talent, which in western culture, has lain dormant for too long. The reasons are fairly clear when you realise that not so long ago even respected and celebrated astronomers were liable to be burned at the stake if they published anything contrary to church dogma. When he discovered that the only practical, mathematical answer to the puzzling movements of the planets was that the earth must revolve round the sun, Copernicus was wise enough to withhold the publication of his theory until near the end of his life. He was condemned as a heretic by a church whose dogma insisted that the earth was the centre of the universe and when old Galileo's work in the early seventeenth century was published confirming that Copernicus was absolutely right, Galileo was taken out by Dominican monk hit-men, through the infamous Inquisition Court set up earlier by the Roman Catholic Church. Under the most appalling threats he was forced into a meaningless recantation of the Copernican theory. Religious beliefs were being challenged and it was small wonder that these advanced thinkers were a little wary of making their new knowledge public. Galileo was accepted back into the church relatively recently, when the inexcusably blinkered religious authorities finally realised that their stance was no longer tenable.

On occasion I've had lively discussions with some of the more tunnel-visioned of the clerical fraternity on the apparent disapproval of dowsing by the church. Another name for dowsing is 'divining', and there are oft-quoted passages in the Bible which fulminate a little about 'divination'.

Many of my friends of the cloth, however, maintain that the references to divination are strictly to do with the old meaning of the word ... the foretelling of the future.

Nothing to do with dowsing.

Nevertheless many of the old fears are still there, and the art should be practised with discretion, particularly in working with earth-energy around churches. If the building was placed on an ancient sacred site, as many of them were, some of the energies can be pretty potent, and a quiet approach when others are present will help avoid offence. You'll probably learn a lot more that way anyway.

Most of us have heard of dowsing to find water, and if that was its sole purpose it would still be a valuable and endlessly intriguing ability.

If anyone had doubts about the accuracy of dowsing to find water, they had only to meet my old friend Don Wilkins. Sadly. Don departed this life, but his expertise in finding water with a hazel twig cut from a hedge is legendary. I had the pleasure of working with him a number of times, and his dowsing ability had developed beyond the physical manifestations of the twig to using a sense which could 'see' where the water was from the side of a field. He worked on the Cornish landscape, where most of the time he had to drill in the most difficult terrain, through great lumps of granite, on the principle of 'No water—no pay'. This meant that he could not afford to be wrong too often. He always checked with the hazel on the fine positioning of the drill before starting and he could then predict with astonishing accuracy the depth he would have to drill, and the final rate of flow of the water in gallons per hour. Sceptics would declare that you could probably find water if you drilled anywhere, and Don, with the rich chuckle of a man who really knew what he was doing, would invite them to go ahead. He had a big heart and would receive them with gentlemanly courtesy when, perhaps slightly chastened, they came back to see him.

Although they don't talk about it much, the water, electricity and gas companies often use dowsers to find lost pipes and cables which are sometimes not accurately marked on their maps. Telephone engineers using the technique can tell the difference between electric and telephone cables although they are made from intrinsically the same materials. Architects and developers reduce digging costs by finding the positions of drainage systems and old foundations. Mining engineers can find adits and tell whether they are dry or full of water, flowing or otherwise. The search for minerals in ever more inaccessible places led to new methods of dowsing from maps.

The list is endless, and the common denominator amongst all of these practitioners is that they have taken the time to fine-hone their minds to tune in very precisely to their target.

These uses apply to the practical business of living, but perhaps the greatest contribution that dowsing can make is still to come. An increasing number of people feel strongly that they have a purpose here beyond mere survival, that coping with 'housekeeping' problems, at whatever level, is not enough. Recent dowsing work with the energies has triggered breathtaking responses from the earth which require a fundamental reappraisal of our relationship with our planet.

Simple Ways to Start

Many fine books have been written on the practice of dowsing, and for anyone starting out on this exciting pilgrimage there are two which, to me, are quite outstanding.

Dowsing. Techniques and Applications by Tom Graves is written with a profound basic knowledge of the skill, with a particularly intuitive understanding of the problems of the beginner, and with the sense of humour and humility which is so essential in progressing dowsing work. His detailed instruction is second to none. The other, by Sig Lonegren, is titled **Spiritual Dowsing** and leads from basic instruction in dowsing through more advanced techniques to the development of personal inner growth.

There are many local groups of dowsers all over the country who meet regularly and welcome beginners at their meeting and outings. There is no better way to learn than working with these enthusiasts who will happily guide you on the basics and set you on your way on the joys of discovery. You can find out where they are through the British Society of Dowsers at their headquarters in Kent. They are extremely active, with a large membership, and have specialists in every field who are always prepared to help with practical demonstrations and advice.

The basic requirements are very simple. It's better to start with a tool of some kind like a pendulum or 'L' rod. The best choice is the one with which you feel most comfortable.

Pendulums can be made from anything with a bit of weight, a wooden turned bob, a favourite ring or locket, a nut and bolt attached to a thread or fine chain. Better to avoid crystals because they can have 'memory' which may confuse answers unless you are very careful.

Rods can be bent from old coat hangers, brazing or welding rod, or, if you want to be upmarket, hand-forged on the anvil by someone who knows what he is doing!

I've been involved in introducing a number of people to earth-energy dowsing and I wish I had photographed the wonderful expressions of awe, delight, surprise and partial disbelief on their faces when they feel the first positive response.

"It's not me! They're moving by themselves!"

They try it again and again to see if it really works, and bursts of incredulous and infectious laughter release any lingering doubts they might have had.

The initial recognition that the tool is reacting from a stimulus within you is profoundly moving, and for many it can be the beginning of a mystical pilgrimage. The length of the journey is a measure of your unique capacity to learn, and the driving force comes from untouched reserves deep in your subconscious.

Take your time to become familiar with the movement of the rods or pendulum.

One of the most serious concerns about the society we live in, is that so many are obsessed with the need for instant results.

I plant lots of little trees, some of them only two inches high, in my rough bit of land in Cornwall and am often confounded by people who seriously question why I do it.

"You'll never see them fully grown," they say ... as if it mattered.

I know what they'll look like when fully matured, and I watch their yearly progress with endless pleasure.

You don't have to wait a lifetime for dowsing to come to fruition, although the learning process never stops. It is, however, necessary to put in a bit of practice in order to get consistent results.

Imagine presenting a piano to someone who had never seen one before. Within moments a pure sound can be made by pressing a finger on one of the white bits. The experience could be expanded by pressing two or three of them together to make a pleasing resonance. Some natural sequences of sound may soon evolve into a simple tune.

It's still an awfully long way from a Rachmaninov Prelude.

Once you have the first response from the piano or the dowsing rod, you must then learn what can be done with it. With the piano an enormous amount of practice, dedication, dexterity with hands, co-ordination of sight, sound and feeling will produce a truly competent musical interpretation. From there it needs a mystical transformation to take the performance into the unique dimension of genius.

With the dowsing rod there is no further stimulation of the five senses after the feeling of movement. The practice and discipline is in training your mind to focus with pin-point accuracy on precisely what you are looking for. You need to reach a state of relaxed concentration. Sounds like a paradox but the concentration is in one particular part of your mind while the relaxation is in everything else.

The most difficult thing for a dowser to learn is how the rational mind must never be allowed to influence results. Time and again I have seen enthusiasts follow a long, false trail after a couple of suspect readings have triggered a new idea. It's very easy to be led astray when your mind is inducing the answers you want to find. No one is ever a hundred per cent right, but the deeper the concentration the more chance you have of being accurate. Phrasing your questions to the rod or pendulum is an exact science and the wording must be structured for a simple 'yes' or 'no' answer. I know some dowsers who get a 'maybe' but I feel that they probably haven't phrased the question properly. If any form of judgement enters the equation, your rational mind will inevitably take over. The only limitations on the art of dowsing are in the ability to ask the right questions, *and the discipline to accept answers that your conditioned mind does not expect.*

In the early stages many dowsers use a 'witness' when working. This is a sample or representation of what you are looking for, held in one hand, or in your teeth if you like, to help you focus. I once worked with a chap who had a thick body belt with more than fifty different minerals and materials hanging from straps so that he could cover any eventuality on a day's march. It worked well, but he didn't half have some problems when he came to a fence or gate. I believe that a witness does help to concentrate the mind and even an expert like Don Wilkins used to make use of a colour wheel ... a three-inch diameter disc with sections printed in different colours ... to help his concentration in ascertaining differing qualities of water more easily. Electricity company engineers often have a chunk of cable the right size clutched in one hand. It depends a lot on an ability to visualise your target really accurately. I don't think it would be necessary or desirable to lug a section of drainpipe around a site since it is a fairly easy thing to concentrate on.

Dowsing Practice.

Ba dowsing the
Tote Stone near
Skiabost in Skye.

When you are dealing with earth energy, however, it is patently not possible to have a sample bottle of the right combination of wavelengths, and you have to develop an internal resonance to the specific frequency, or band of frequencies, for which you are searching.

I found it particularly difficult at first to differentiate between the various lines of force which activated the rods. It seemed as though there was a baffling and impossible number of reactions, which were much too complex to rationalise. Gradually, however, I became aware of certain continuities and interactions which led to the first glimmerings of understanding a very small part of the system.

Chapter Eleven

DOWSING AND EARTH-ENERGY

As my first tentative attempts to look for earth energy lines were on Trencrom Hill it seemed a good place to find out a little more. I had found the line connecting the Hill to St Michael's Mount by walking slowly across the lower slopes, holding the rods in front of me like the Sundance Kid and asking them to show me if it was there.

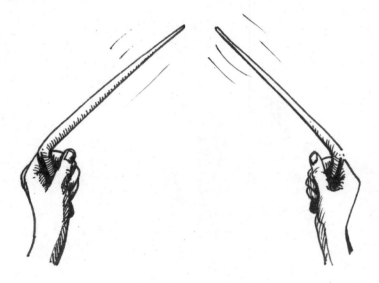

... Holding the rods like the Sundance Kid ...

The 'walking slowly', I recognise now, is quite fundamental in the interpretation of subtle energy lines. That time I was forced to do it because the brambles were the fiercest, thickest and most tenacious I've ever come across. The line, of course, went right through the middle of the patch. Over the years we have observed considerable influences on plant life on or near energy lines. We have, sitting happily near the cottage, a gigantic clump of what we affectionately call our man-eating primroses, which seem to turn their huge yellow heads round to watch as we pass.

I've seen dowsers marching determinedly, rods and pendulums whistling round like propellers through a veritable web of energy lines, proudly proclaiming...

"Yes. There's something here! I wonder what it is?"

In the first place the dowser should *know* what he has found because he should be looking for something specific, and secondly, he should move slowly in order to receive accurate signals. I use 'he' with the clear understanding that 'she' is included as a fifty percent partner, and I find the politically correct 'he/she' irritating if constantly repeated.

I had asked whether the energy line existed and had received a positive response indicating where it was. I wanted to know the width of the band, and asked the rods to show me the nearest and farthest edge of the energy as I walked across it. The rods turned at one spot and I marked the position with a small cane. Once the rods have turned you have to point them to the front again. A slow pace or two forward and another turn of the rods showed that the line was about a metre wide. The signal seemed to be very weak and I got no response to my question as to whether it was one solid band of energy. I asked if it was made up of separate lines of energy and, on their slow passage over the metre width, the rods indicated that there were five barely perceptible single lines. Further dowsing showed that three of those, the centre and two outers, flowed in one direction while the two inners were reversed. To find direction, hold the rods in front of you over the energy line, with your hands touching, the handles close together, and ask if the flow is to the right or the left. Both rods will turn simultaneously in the direction of the current.

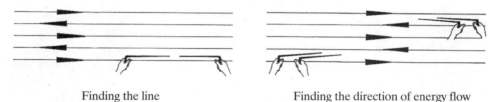

Finding the line · · · · · · · · · · · · · Finding the direction of energy flow

As the months passed it became obvious that either the line was becoming stronger, or I was developing a greater sensitivity. It became much easier to pick up, and after a session in Sussex working with the very experienced energy dowser, Roger Brown from Adelaide, Australia, I became aware that some of the lines in the band responded to a visualisation of different colours. It was the earth's gentle way of telling us thick humans that they were of different frequencies.

Back in Cornwall checking on my local line I found to my astonishment that the width had increased to two metres, and that it was now made up of twelve separate bands. The colour spread was a mirror image starting from the centre, but not in the normal rainbow sequence.

Progressively the width increased to include more and more separate lines which started to band together forming stronger 'ribbons', each responding to differing colours. At this time it became apparent that the direction of energy flow, while remaining constant in one coloured ribbon, tended to reverse at certain times. While there was always a flow in both directions throughout the line, the predominance of movement would be towards St Michael's Mount in the evening, and a reversal of this in the morning. At each stage of discovery I used to feel that I was well on the way to making a significant breakthrough in the understanding of the earth energy system, but time after time I was led gently on to the next step.

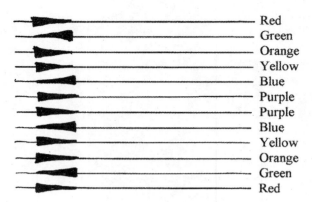

Individual lines in the band have different frequencies

The ribbons near the centre gradually stopped responding to particular colours and while there were some additional responses to visualisations of gold, silver and white, there remained an increasing number of bands in the middle which, although dowsable as energy lines, did not respond to concepts of colour. It was a long time before I discovered that some of them occasionally reacted to abstract concepts like love, anger and fear, the dowsing reaction depending on the quality of the visualisation. The centre pair remained inert until I happened on the thought of 'ancient knowledge'. The response was immediate and powerful, and I thought I had plugged in to the global consciousness. In great excitement I found a comfortable place to hunker down in the middle of the line, took some deep breaths, calmed my mind and moved into a meditative state. Thinking that at last I might have cracked it, I indicated that I was ready for any revelations.

"No. You're not!" came a kind but disconcertingly firm message in my mind, "You've still got a long way to go."

Something or someone was trying very hard to communicate, but the crude basic five senses available to me could not begin to cope with the subtleties of their language. I remembered the difficulties the Americans had with attempts to contact dolphins. These beautiful creatures have a number of highly sophisticated levels of aural communication with each other. These are made much more complex by variations in meaning expressed by simultaneous body posture, and apparently they automatically revert to their equivalent of 'baby' language in order to get down to our level. I suppose the equivalent the other way round would be our attempting to chat with a sea slug.

Where do you *start*?

I realised I had to develop my own perceptions a great deal before the Management would reveal anything significant.

The work Colin Bloy had been doing in dowsing earth grids, the energy manifestations around healers, and the related 'earth healing' Fountain Group was an inspiration to research this field. He had found that when the healing process was applied by a group of people to a place rather than a person, the grid for some considerable distance around was affected by the group energy. He also found that the alterations in the earth energy field had a considerably calming effect on the behaviour of the people in the area. In addition to changes in the grid the electromagnetic fields manifested some very specific shapes, a few of which are illustrated below. Some of these first manifestations are familiar and reflect the symbolism from an number of ancient cultures. Others have a direct connection with 12th century Templar activity.

Templar Connections

As the shapes changed to more complex structures we began to realise that they were a kind of response display from the earth to the work we were doing.

At this time I was working with friends in the National Federation of Spiritual Healers and had their OK to dowse their sanctuaries before and after the healing process, to see if any pattern was common to them all. One interesting factor became apparent after I had checked dozens of these in different areas of the country.

In each case a regular grid pattern would form, the size depending not only on how long the healer had been using the room, but also on the quality of the healing. It varied enormously in various parts of the U.K. and the few observations which I managed to make abroad seemed to confirm that the effects were the same world-wide. There appeared to be a quietly pulsing universal square or rectangular earth grid-pattern, sometimes with more than a hundred metres between the lines, and in other areas with just a few centimetres.

From my own experience, from Colin, and from a number of independent sources, there was a general agreement that it was possible to dowse a fluctuating grid pattern of energy which seemed to cover large areas of the surface of the planet. There were, and still are, a number of interpretations of this grid, some of which have been claimed by particular dowsers to have very specific dimensions and positions. Amongst these are the Hartmann and Curry grids, named after the dowsers who discovered them. My strong feeling is that each one is picking up a marginally different aspect of the live, pulsing grid which is the equivalent of the earth's nervous and/or meridian system. It is immensely complex and works at levels which suggest that we do not yet have nearly enough data to pin it down. It certainly will never be resolved by a simple set of coordinates.

Since my apprenticeship with established National Federation practitioners I had been using my cottage for healing, and it gave me the opportunity to do some long-term research on the behaviour of the earth's magnetic fields around an area where healing was regularly practised. I had seen some astonishing photographic evidence of the movement of other energies and was intrigued to find out more about it.

Matthew Manning, one of the most powerful and effective healers in this country, has a series of photographs taken by Professor Owen and Doctor Wolfson at a Research Foundation in Canada, using an ordinary black and white Polaroid camera. As Matthew attuned himself to the healing mode the sequence shows a build-up of energy starting from his hands and finally encompassing his whole body. The final shots show a positive transfer of energy from himself to the patient. Matthew has patiently undergone controlled experiment after experiment with scientific and medical authorities across the globe in an attempt to prise open their sceptical minds in matters relating to the use of natural energies. The results are invariably so contrary to accepted practice that the examiners end up accusing each other of falsifying records, or, more seriously, of professional incompetence.

Meanwhile Matthew quietly goes on, spreading the practice and knowledge of his healing and special talents in the use of subtle energies.

I suppose the medical 'experts' are no worse than the aerodynamic boffins who put up an extremely good case to prove that a bumble bee can't fly.

The extraordinary photograph of an energy field opposite was taken in Russia near the border with Finland by the extremely sensitive lady who organised our trip. It was the fifth in a series of twelve shots and none of the other prints was affected by any malfunction of the camera. We were checking some results for one of the Russian dowsing programmes and had arrived on the edge of the estate at a tiny building which seemed to be right on the most powerful energy centre in the area. Our translator suddenly felt very dizzy and unwell and asked if she could have some healing. During the process the photograph was taken for no other reason than to record the moment, and somehow Molly Hegarty caught the energy flow on the negative. I have a collection now of photographs of similar happenings but this was the only occasion in which I was personally involved. It needs a special state of mind behind the camera to capture these phenomena, and although I have tried many times to take shots at times when I feel the energy is present, the very act of 'trying' seems to inhibit any positive results.

Russian Energy   MOLLY HEGARTY

THE EARTH RESPONDS

As a test case I decided to check out the grid outside the cottage and compare it with any variations inside the building where the healing usually took place. Dowsing the grid lines showed that the size on the lawn at this time was approximately two by one and a half metres and for reference I marked this out with some old canes. This enabled me to photograph the grid from the upstairs window and I have a pictorial record of the variations over a period of a number of weeks.

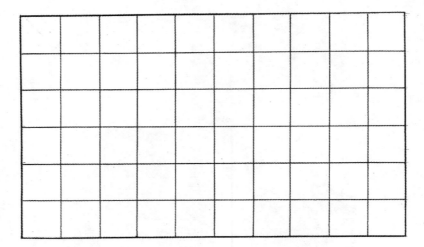

Earth Grid 1

At the same time some interesting things were happening inside. The grid started off about half the size of the one outside but very rapidly reduced in size as I worked with it. The experiment lasted a number of weeks and I decided to concentrate on the inside since most of the action seemed to be taking place there.

Over the period the grid gradually reduced until it was approximately 100 millimetres square. It then became quite difficult to differentiate the separate lines as they got closer and closer and, rather than laboriously counting each line, I learned to do 'ratio' dowsing by asking the rods to show me every tenth or fiftieth line. It's a very quick way of finding how many individual lines are in an energy band.

One evening I noticed a subtle change in the formation of the grid. Instead of forming an even spread over the floor some of the lines started to concentrate closer together in two areas, one approximately north/south and the other east/west.

These changes led to one of the most moving, profound experiences I have ever had on this earth.

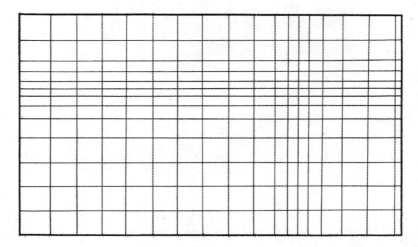

Earth Grid 2

As they concentrated ever closer it became almost impossible to distinguish between the separate energy lines. It was an exciting time and each day I dowsed the changes not knowing quite why I was doing it, but eager to find out what it all meant.

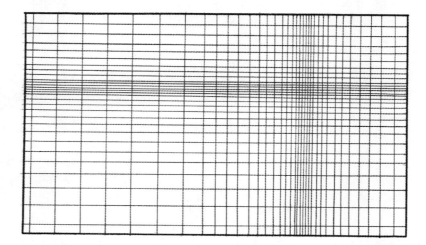

Earth Grid 3

So it was with a terrible sense of loss, that I came in one evening, during a partial eclipse of the moon, and found no dowsing reactions at all. Concentrate as I might, I could find absolutely nothing. My first reaction was that perhaps I couldn't dowse any more, and to me it was the equivalent of losing an arm or a leg. The extra sense developed by dowsers becomes as much a part of their being as any of their physical bits.

For nearly two hours I checked and rechecked, coming ever closer to real despair ... then suddenly I got a positive movement from the rod. I whooped with pure joy and started checking the grid.

There was something different about the reactions but, in my relief, I didn't notice anything at first. Then I saw that the rod was pulling towards one

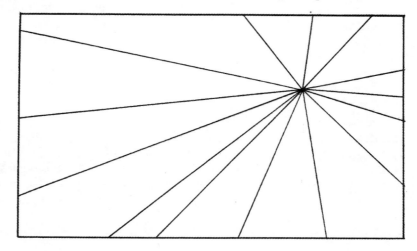

Radials from the energy centre

particular point in the room. It was exactly where the concentrated sections of lines had crossed, and the grid had given way to another energy manifestation. Painfully slowly I located new lines which now seemed to be coming from a common centre. There were fourteen of them, unevenly spaced and coming out from the centre like the spokes of a bicycle wheel. I wanted to keep a reference on this first manifestation and marked each one on the carpet with masking tape.

Where the 'bunching' occurred they seemed to form a line or band which left the vortex and went through the walls of the cottage to the outside. On dowsing there I found the energy joining to other centres and feeding to larger and stronger bands in a continuous and complex network like tributaries flowing into a mighty river.

Some time later I was pondering on the significance of the change when it occurred to me to check for any other energy patterns round the centre. Again not quite knowing what I was doing, I dowsed along the length of each radial towards the centre, poking the end of the dowsing rod to make a hole through the tape wherever I got a reaction. I didn't go round in sequence but started from arbitrary directions.

It was pretty confusing.

There seemed to be different numbers of holes on some of the radials with random distances between. I sat on a chair and looked at it from a distance. No flicker of understanding. I walked over and looked down on it from a position above the centre.

I have never seen anything quite so exquisitely beautiful as the perfect spiral below me. As a blacksmith I often work with these forms, but I could never have created this flawless symmetry. I looked, hair rising on the back of my neck, with the awesome realisation that the earth had used this outline of a basic building block of the universe to respond to the stimulation of one of her very minor energy centres. She had used the field fluctuations from the effects of the eclipse to manifest the change.

I felt close to her, part of her, and could feel her gentle rebuke at the way we have been treating her. The joy of recognising her communication was tinged with sadness, tears recognising the enormity of the task we have if we are to change our collective thinking to recognise her for what she is.

I sat, far into the night, stunned by the implications behind this simple but eloquent indication that the earth is aware of each one of us and everythin was also a practical confirmation that dowsing can lead to the exponential expansion of our perceptions.

I worked for long hours with the spiral, getting to know her moods and variations at different times of day and night. Nuances of change with moon cycles, sun activity, planetary influences ... all had subtle effects on her behaviour. The feeling, however, that seemed to trigger the biggest responses was the sense of communication between us. As soon as this was established ... (and I was always the one who was way behind ... remember the sea slug?) ... she started to react in ever more complex ways.

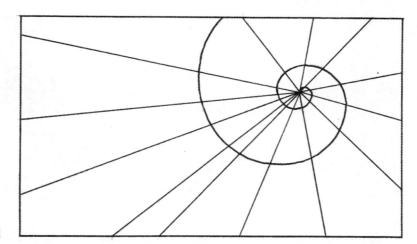

The first
exquisite spiral

She would tighten up like a clock spring when I started dowsing and end up with several turns where there had been only a couple a few minutes before. At a slightly different level of dowsing, perhaps tuned to this new interaction, she would add dozens of new radials from the centre, incorporating the original fourteen and filling in the spaces between them. They were always bunched in certain directions and sparse in others. These seemed to be almost infinitely variable while the original fourteen have stayed precisely where they first appeared.

One evening I made the usual check to find what the spiral was doing. My rod seemed to be more than normally active and I restarted a careful marking of each reaction on the fourteen radials, again out of sequence so that it was impossible to predetermine any result. I was a bit disappointed in the end to find a jumble of random dots which meant nothing at all.

I got the feeling then very like the one I get now, when my word processor starts to swallow things and print gobble-de-gook endlessly until I have to switch it off in a desperate attempt to stop it using up another pine tree. I know it's capable of doing wonderful things, and it's all my fault, but at the moment with my very basic knowledge I am not really able to cope.

I sat ruminating, idly sipping a measure of the world's finest vegetarian tincture. Lagavulin is the ultimate nectar, and the island of Islay was indeed blessed by the gods when they decided it should be produced there. Perhaps there was a tiny shift in my perception when I looked again at the confusion of points.

There was a second spiral inside the first, equally beautiful, starting from the same point and moving out in perfect symmetry with its partner.

If I had not been convinced by the first, deciding that it must have been a coincidence, a happy accident, or contrived from my own consciousness, I had to accept now that it was a simple, definitive and very positive response from the earth's living system. There is no possible way that this new manifestation could have come from me. The pure joy of my own response, the appreciation of the exquisite natural form, poured out in an uninhibited expression of surprise, welcome and relief that at last here was a bridge on which we could build a new rapport.

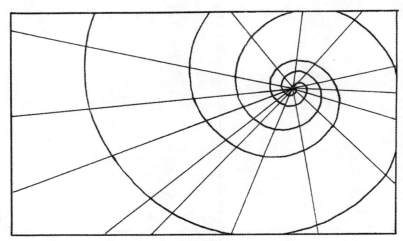

A second spiral
inside the first

The energy centre works at a level which encompasses knowledge and senses aeons beyond mine, but has nevertheless managed to guide me by symbolism and gentle intuitive nudging towards a clearer understanding of our relationship with the earth.

I had delved into some of the old Druid legends and found a 'knowing' that there are twelve major lines of force circling the earth. They are not necessarily great circles, and the points where they meet and cross are potentially very powerful energy centres. Many of these are recognised sacred sites. Some have not yet been found, some have been desecrated, all of them are active in varying degrees. These circular cords of energy are the earth's equivalent of the meridians in our body, with connections through various organs to its nervous system. What I learned from the energy centre was that the lines could divide and subdivide like the tributaries of a river until the entire surface of the earth was interlaced with tiny but sensitive centres like the nerve endings in our fingertips.

The other week in the forge I burned myself on the underside of my forearm, a place which seldom is affected by anything I do. It was stupid, of course. I had laid aside some long pieces with preliminary work done, ready to finish, and they were still hot. I reached up on tip toe to adjust a wire cable, swinging my arm back to balance myself. As my arm touched the hot metal, one little nerve ending which had been sitting doing absolutely nothing for sixty nine years suddenly fired up and sent a swift message to my brain to get my muscles to pull the arm away. It was very efficient and saved any serious damage.

My earth energy centre tells me that it feels the same way as the little nerve ending. There are countless millions of them, all interconnected, and because they developed with the titanic forces of creation when the earth's crust was formed, and are not transient beings like us, they can wait pulsing happily for sixty nine *million* years before they are stimulated into action. Time doesn't mean quite the same thing to them as it does to us. They each have a sense of belonging and being a tiny part of the whole. They are aware of their easy contact with the cosmos and all things and beings within it. They are part of the energy of the universe and because of that they have access to all information from all time. They are a cosmic internet on a scale that makes our latest stuff look like two bean tins with a bit of string between them.

But they are also aware of the fragility of the system, and are concerned to access our minds. They need to get through to us so that we begin to care once more. The old people knew the importance of the delicate balances of nature and ecological systems, and it is still not too late for us to accept the profound need for that clear understanding again.

Each interconnected energy band has the capacity to carry an almost infinite number of messages but also has characteristics of its own. A look at the constitution of the band width shows that each one contains a different number of individual lines of force with differing directions of travel. To complicate matters further each individual line has its own frequency. It seems to create a gigantic problem of identification, but the characteristics provide one method of identifying a particular line by creating a 'signature' that is unique.

It is possible to use these variations to tune into a sort of 'chord' of vibrations which expresses the 'personality' of the line. I use the word deliberately because there are ramifications implied in the structure of each line which go beyond the simple analysis of frequency. Ba had been working on a way to get herself in resonance with this strange quality of an energy line. One morning she traced part of a powerful line through the Penwith and found a quiet place on the cliffs where it disappeared into the sea. She took off her shoes to make real contact with the earth and slowly drifted into a meditative state, her whole being tuned to the pulsing energies around her. For some time there seemed to be no response, then faintly but with growing intensity a murmuring harmonic chord impinged on her senses. She realised that she wasn't 'hearing' the sound but rather feeling it through her bones. For a long time she sat, feeling the joy of the earth's communication, absorbing the special imprint of the energy line.

Later she talked of the deep rapport she found with the earth during her meditation and although she knows that she can't reproduce the 'sound' by voice or instrument, some internal mechanism now allows her to detect that line anywhere amongst a thousand other similar ones. On one occasion we had travelled many hundreds of miles in the car when Ba felt the first whispers of the 'chord'. It became stronger as we progressed and I confess on that occasion my rational mind had told me that the line couldn't be there. Finally the feeling almost reached the pain level and we stopped to check with the rods. We found it about fifty yards behind the car. It had curved out round an ancient site unknown to us at the time and had crossed the road at a point which we couldn't possibly have predicted.

Perhaps it explains why the aborigines never seem to get lost in their 'walkabouts' in the desert. To them, following an energy line is as easy as we find walking a country lane. We use our sight to follow the path. They use more highly developed senses which we completely failed to recognise when we first met them. And because we didn't understand them, what did we do? *We* called *them* ignorant savages.

This tuning in to a specific energy line takes a bit of practice, and unless you develop a considerable degree of concentration, you can be diverted by the joining of a similar tributary to the main line. The process is infinitely rewarding because you become conscious of a very special rapport with one part of the earth's living system.

It can't be more difficult than a penguin finding its chick by the 'shape' of its squeak amongst all that mass of squalling bird life, or a bat finding its mate in a pitch black cave with millions of 'identicals' hanging from the roof ... upside down as well.

LEY LINES

Strictly speaking a ley line is the straight connection of at least four sacred or significant sites, after Alfred Watkins' vision as he was pounding around the countryside on his horse. The longer ones have to be adjusted by the equivalent of rhumb line sailing to allow for the curvature of the earth, and a computer programme has been devised to do this. A great deal has been written about these and a lot of people have fun finding new ones on maps. There are some very significant line-ups, and there are doubtless thousands of interesting ones to be found locally. The *Ley Hunter* has what should be an interesting and exciting remit for the study of ley lines, earth energy and all its ramifications, and it seems a pity that the lugubrious past and present proprietors seem reduced to deriving their energy from the vilification, over the last decade, of everyone who has made contributions which don't happen to coincide with their own views. Ley Lines are the obvious pointers to something more important, and we are just beginning to discover the deeper meanings of our relationship with the earth through its energy responses

ENERGY LINES

Energy lines weave, spiralling sometimes, then flow naturally in pairs, crossing at special places, finally connecting everything and everyone to the twelve great pulsing spinal cords round the earth. They are the Serpents of legend, Dragons to the Chinese, Wouivres to the French, and they provide our direct connection through the angelic forces to the universe. They move gently amongst us, nudging our senses to become aware of them, and are waiting for us to recognise them.

In most cases these are the lines involved when people say ...

"I have a *ley line* running through my house."

They have a profound effect on our behaviour. In common with the mineral, plant and animal life of our planet we are surrounded by electro and biomagnetic fields like onion skins beyond our bodies. They are extremely subtle and delicately balanced and are responsive to variations from all external fields. The most familiar is the 'aura', which some people can see, and which surrounds us like a sort of space suit taking up the general shape of our body. It's easily dowsed with rod, pendulum or the fingers. With the rod it can be found from fifteen to thirty inches from the body depending on the strength of the field, and with practice the strength and contour can be used as a guide for healing. Where the field is weak there tends to be a resulting problem in the physical body, and it is sometimes possible to detect and prevent a health problem by checking the auric field. If I use my hand, my arthritic old blacksmith's fingers are not as sensitive as the rod, but I can still detect the aura two or three inches from the body. It feels like a very soft balloon and I think what I get is the reaction of another auric field on my own.

Kirlian photography has shown even the cynics that we have little energy streams coming out from each of our fingers. The good news is that this can be used and directed on to weak auric or any other biomagnetic fields to build them up. It's a bit like sculpturing soft plaster. Point your fingers like a pistol and you will begin to feel the flow, then gently mould the energy body with the flat of your hand. People can actually feel sensations around the related organs and it can be a very effective healing.

CHAKRAS

Seven other important biomagnetic fields are commonly known as the 'chakras', a name pinched from Eastern practitioners.

Much has also been written about these fields and it is sufficient here to establish that they, also, are profoundly affected by the influence of surrounding energies.

Basically the first four - from the bottom up - base, spleen, solar plexus and heart, should be circular and centred on your spine.

I have dowsed many hundreds of these and have yet to find a set which has not been battered about a bit by our current life-style. Some of them have lumps out like wedges from a cheese; some are like doughnuts with four bites out of the rim; some have bulges where they shouldn't and nothing where they should; and some are way off-centre. They can be treated in the same sculptural way, rather like the wheel of a car when you stick weights on one side to get the dynamic balance right, and because of my profession I tend to visualise welding them into permanent equilibrium once they are shaped up and centred.

The Seven Main Chakras

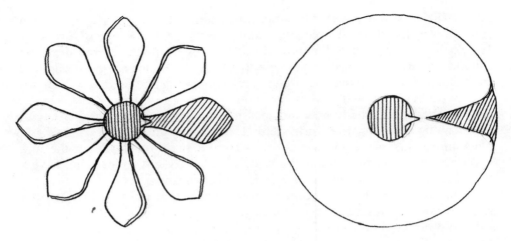

Solar Plexus energy

I worked once with a healing lady who could 'see' chakras in colour. On one occasion we decided, with the client's permission, to check our findings on his solar plexus energy field. Her treatment centre was three miles away, and we arranged that I should dowse remotely from my cottage, tuning to the chakra at a prearranged time. The results were significant. We exchanged sketches before we talked about what we had found, and while she had 'seen' a full, yellow flowerlike energy with one petal at the front in reddish brown, I had picked up the circular shape with a wedge out of the front lacking in any energy response.

The other three main energy fields are around the throat, the pineal gland or 'third eye', and the crown. The first one is interesting. It's about communication, naturally, with the vocal chords just behind it, but there's a lot more to it. It can be dowsed with a rod or pendulum and my records seem to show that most people are quietly probing for an alternative means of interaction beyond our standard aural interpretation of grunting noises. In fact I'll go as far as to say that we will *have* to develop an alternative method of communication which

Communications

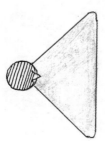

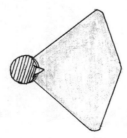
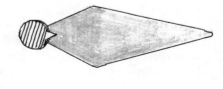

Normal throat chakra   Awakening throat chakra   Active throat chakra

does not depend on language alone before we really get going on the next major evolutionary cycle. Below are illustrations of the shape of the throat chakra for people with differing communicative talents. The first is the shape that most of us have, the second seems to develop when we home in on a possible new way of exchanging ideas, and the third evolves when we become clairaudient, clairsentient or clairvoyant.

I find difficulty checking the field from the third eye with rods and use both hands in the same way as checking the aura. You can feel the edges like a soft balloon, the energy from right brain registering on the left and vice versa.

The sketch clarifies the shape and it is interesting to find how the balance of activity changes in the same person at different times of the day when they are more involved in the practical business of coping with day-to-day problems, and when in more relaxed creative or intuitive mood.

Right and left brain energy from the third eye.

The crown is a great joy and gives a very revealing insight into spiritual connections. I use 'spiritual' in the widest sense of the word, i.e. the vital principle or life force within living beings. Again difficult to dowse with anything other than the hands, it can take many forms. The first, where there is little or no activity, barely discernible like a close fitting skull cap; then through a series of progressively larger bowler hats without the rims, to a full-blown witch's hat. A few have an open tube with straight sides. You can feel the shapes with the fingers and, with your client's permission, you can add or subtract energy from the field and mould it to improve their potential to make contact with higher levels of beings.

   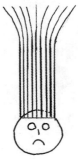

Crown Chakras

From experience it seems that a well balanced crown chakra is in the shape of a witch's or wizard's hat, and there is little doubt that the original concept of its shape came from people who could see the energy field. It's interesting that when healers are working, their crown chakra opens up like a tube to receive whatever energy they are using, but if it doesn't close up (leaving a little hole at the top to enable you to keep an eye on things) you tend to get an overload of etheric input equivalent to listening to a dozen radio stations at once. It's tiring and it certainly makes no sense. I've checked one or two people whose crown chakra was like a daffodil ... a great trumpet catching all sorts of energies from the cosmos. In each case the relief from the change to a conical hat was likened to switching off Heavy Metal from a ghetto blaster ... bliss!

Upsetting these incredibly delicate biomagnetic fields around us can give rise to the health problems referred to in a previous chapter. Dowsing has given us an insight to the nature of the problems and can perhaps guide us to broader solutions once we realise the full extent to which electromagnetic and industrial pollution are affecting our quality of life.

A Few Steps Further

Tracing the network from the cottage, starting with the very small lines that sprouted from the energy centre where the radials were 'bunching', led me to wander further afield. The natural progression was, of course, to the standing stones, wells, burial mounds, sacred sites, ancient villages and stone circles which proliferate in the area of the Penwith.

One of the first experiences I had was to set standards of behaviour in this field of research in no uncertain terms. I had been following various lines all day and ended up dowsing one of the small stones in a lane near The Merry Maidens. I was checking the number of radials from the stone to see that, in common with most of the ones I'd checked nearby, it had the basic twenty ... par for the course in this part of the country. Perhaps I was a bit tired and was a little cavalier in my treatment of the stone. I leaned on it with my left hand and immediately felt the equivalent of a belting electric shock coursing up through to my shoulder. It was not quite the same as one from the mains, but was sufficient to prevent me from driving for a quarter of an hour after getting back to the car. I couldn't work my left arm muscles to grip the steering wheel or change gear. The next day I went back to apologise, and now the stone and I are the best of friends. It was interesting to read later that Tom Graves had the same kind of experience once when he was thrown to the ground in similar circumstances. It is the earth's way of getting the priorities right from the start, and if you are going to get anywhere in this work you have to treat the whole system with a great deal of respect.

The stone circle known as the Merry Maidens is set in a field near a main road. Access is relatively easy and the constant stream of visitors may contribute to the fact that the energy seems to be considerably muted during the day. There are nineteen stones in the circle and the energy centre is about four feet

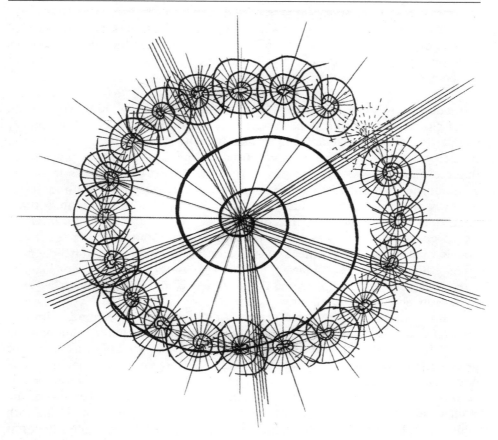

Merry Maidens' Energy

west of the geometric centre. From this centre a series of twenty radials is marked accurately by the stones, the twentieth passing slightly to the right of the centre of the gap which is usually taken to be the entrance. I feel that there was another stone there originally, marking the twentieth radial. There is a spiral or vortex of energy winding out from the centre, similar to but much bigger than the one in my cottage, and each individual stone has its own configuration of twenty radials and spiral. A number of quite significant energy lines join the site to neighbouring centres and this complex structure is only part of the whole story. Small wonder that dowsers find it difficult to interpret much of what is happening at these sacred sites. There is also some confusion as to whether the energy fields are related to underground streams of water. In some cases water is related to energy fields but generally speaking the flow has little bearing on the complex structures of the earth field. Perhaps some confusion arose from the incredibly detailed work of Guy Underwood whose legendary dowsing was at first for water courses. When he started picking up earth energy he quite understandably attributed this to a function of water, giving his findings names like 'blind springs', and there are still dowsers who believe that earth energy fields are created in some way by water. The sketch illustrates the complexity of the comparatively simple fields round the stones and when the interconnections with the outer system are included it begins to come clear that a supercomputer will be needed to analyse the interactions.

In addition to these lines, the Merry Maidens site, in common with all the other circles I have dowsed, has a series of eight concentric circles of energy round the circumference, encompassing all of the stones. I thought for a long time that these were a sort of 'protection' and perhaps, in a way, they are. A fuller explanation is that they are a form of sensor which tunes in to the consciousness of any being approaching the circle. If we enter with the right intent, with a reverence for the sacred site, and at least the beginnings of an understanding of its meaning, the circle switches on, responding to our thoughts and preparing us for a change in perceptions. Without question it reflects openly what we have in our heads, and the different responses that people have on entering the circle are an insight into the state of their mind. Fear of so many things has a powerful influence on the way we live, and in these places we tend to be more acutely aware of our weaknesses.

At night the circle seems to relax its tight daytime discipline. Close to midnight on a full moon, I went there to pay my respects and meditate at the centre. It was one of those crisp wintry nights with the wind blowing small but dense clouds across the face of the moon as I sat prepared for anything. I was hoping, at the time, for a meeting with Pan, who was a lovely chap before he was given such a bad press by one of the religious cults. The light flickered over the stones and I had a great feeling of peace, alone in the sense of not being with people, but joyfully at one with the entire universe. For some time I hovered between worlds. Pan was otherwise engaged that night, but I caught the feeling that I should move from the centre to the outside of the circle. I was drawn to one particular stone and stood with my arms round it almost feeling the sporadic crackling cross-connections between it and all the others.

I suddenly became aware of movement at the energy centre. The clouds had gone and the moonlight was clear and white. It was vague at first, a sort of sandy gold-coloured something which changed shape as I watched. It became clearer when I looked slightly to one side so that the energy centre was partly in peripheral vision. A series of slowly changing geometric shapes was manifesting, never greater than a metre high and perhaps half a metre wide. There seemed to be a vertical containment of the movement on each side like miniature gold rugby posts, but inside that, balletic changes of shape from circle to ovoid to meniscus to parabola. The sketches are an attempt to give an impression of what I saw, but can't hope to express the joy of the experience.

The strange movements lasted several minutes, giving me a number of chances to look away, blink, adjust and, earthbound, convince myself that it was just a trick of light. Each time I looked back it was still there, an effortless, eloquent display of the meeting of synchronous earth-energies. As it gradually

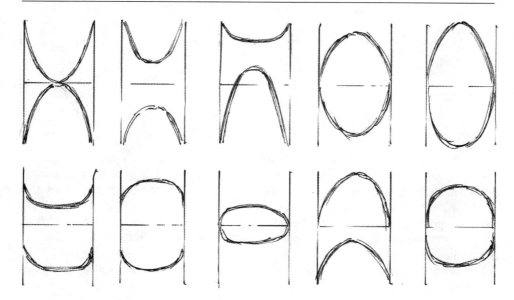

Merry Maidens' Dance

faded I was reminded of the legend of the circle ... that originally the stones were a group of girls who committed the terrible crime of dancing on the Sabbath and were turned to stone for their sins.

I had seen the real dance of the stones.

I treasured the experience for years, the manifestations staying in the back of my mind along with so many other things that needed some confirmation. I was with a group in St Austell one evening and was attracted by sounds from the other side of the room. A young American was sitting with a number of white opaque bowls, stroking their rims with a small rubber hammer. Each one was producing beautiful clear musical notes, and I asked him where on earth he got them.

"Oh!" he said, "they're just rejects from some project NASA was on. They probably cost millions of dollars."

His partner, sitting quietly beside him, smiled...

"I'm very glad they made them," she said, "because I can see what the notes are saying."

She was from California and perhaps they are sometimes a little less inhibited than we are. I asked her if she would draw what she saw, and as a succession of pure sounds poured from the bowls she did some rapid sketching.

She passed them over to me, and I went very still and quiet when I looked at her work.

She had produced a series of perfect replicas of the Merry Maidens dance.

Chapter Twelve

VISION OF THE SERPENT

HAVING BEEN convinced by dowsing, seeing, and feeling some of the more exotic manifestations from the fusions of differing energy-frequencies, I found it a natural step to look further into the work Colin Bloy had initiated in the development of the Fountain Group. With the classically simple idea of applying the group energy of pure love, the fundamental glue of the universe, to the most active energy centre or Hara of an area or town in order to balance the energies, Colin had re-awakened ancient knowledge which has been suppressed for a very long time. The effect of this process is that everyone in the locality has their biomagnetic fields massaged into a more reasonable state of equilibrium.

You may ask what possible difference that can make.

Take the base chakra...

Nothing wrong with a good healthy biomagnetic field around there. It's the earthy-energy of the will to live, of the need to survive, of the importance of sex . It is also the seat of envy, anger, and frustration. Base energy is pumped at us unceasingly by media advertising, pop music, and stimulation by visual image in film and video, and the constant pressure can sometimes lead to overload. When the chakra is in this state, the excess spills over into aggression and violence, and our social problems begin to make themselves felt. If we can learn to move some of this energy upwards through the chakras until it reaches the higher level of the heart, it will increase our capacity for caring, and perhaps cause the 'change of heart' necessary to stop someone chucking yet another brick through a window.

In the twelfth and thirteenth centuries, the Templars were very aware of the influences of subtle energies. Much has been written about these dedicated Knights, with various religious bodies vying in condemnation of their behaviour. They were concerned that if Templar knowledge became available to the masses it would be much more difficult to perpetuate their carefully constructed fear-ridden religious power. The Templars were searching for 'The Holy Grail' and there are as many interpretations of the nature of this ethereal Chalice as there have been researchers. My own feeling is that the essence of the Grail is in the ancient knowledge taught by Mystery Schools since prehistory.

According to many well-informed academics who are now applying a greater degree of lateral thinking to their disciplines, there is growing acceptance that all is not well with current archaeological chronology. In too many cases, conflicting evidence in the dating of sophisticated physical structures and artefacts leads to a blackout in information from whatever authority is defending its position. There are obvious examples like the Valley Temple in Egypt with its stepped and L-shaped cornerstones of up to two hundred tons fitting precisely and without damage. The construction requires lifting and moving these monoliths in a very confined space and the dating shows that the temple was probably constructed a few thousand years before the pyramids.

A confirmation of the dating would indicate that somewhere around ten or eleven thousand BCE there existed a race with a knowledge of building technology far in advance of anything we have now. I understand that research has been stopped in the area by the Egyptian authorities and the temple is gradually being buried in sand. The tragedy is that there is simply not enough money to carry out effective maintenance of the vast number of important sites in Egypt, and they are working on the premise that the sand will probably protect the sites naturally for posterity rather more effectively than they could with limited funds. As the decision on the sites to be preserved is taken by the existing archaeological hierarchy it leaves me with the uncomfortable feeling that any controversial site which perhaps may not conform to comfortable academic theory might suffer the fate of dust pushed under the carpet. The content of the Qumran scrolls is of huge import to people throughout the world who are concerned about the truth behind religious stories, and after half a century the translations are *still* not available because of religious wrangling and academic posturing.

There is a pretty convincing theory that the Sphinx is many thousands of years older than we thought, because the erosion at its base seems to have been caused by water. In fact there is a plethora of evidence in the form of ancient chronometers, batteries, model boats and even aircraft, which lends credence to the existence of an early race on our planet who had knowledge which, in many ways, surpassed ours. In legend they are The Shining Ones and there's an interesting debate on where on earth they lived, if indeed they did exist. The stories of Mu and Atlantis, and the movement of survivors to the Middle East after the disasters, partly explain the sudden acquisition of knowledge in Egypt at that time. An interesting theory of Charles Hapgood's in his work on 'earth crust displacement' suggests that around thirteen thousand years ago the land mass of Antarctica was a couple of thousand miles further north than it is now. A lot of Shining Ones could have lived there in its pleasant subtropical climate. Today, scientists working on the ice cap confirm that the ice thickness is building in some places year on year. If in ancient times, a similar buildup had happened, off centre to the earth's axis of spin, it could have caused a dynamic imbalance, or precession which might have triggered a shift in the earth's crust. Technically it's quite feasible because the crust is thin and hard, and the mantle below is a sort of mobile jelly. Bit like a rounded avocado pear, really. You can imagine if it was whistling round at speed and developed a wobble, in certain circumstances the skin might come loose. There would be no damage to the stone, the mighty core of the planet, and very little to the flesh, or mantle, but the outside of the crusty skin would be a disaster area, specially if some places got stuck. Hence Hapgood believes that Antarctica, which had been enjoying a temperate climate, suddenly and catastrophically shifted thirty degrees south and was frozen stiff overnight. There could be few survivors of such a cataclysm and the remains of the Shining Ones and their knowledge may still be buried under a mile or two of ice near the South Pole. The theory also gives a pretty good reason why, if the northern ice suddenly shifted down, the poor old mammoths up in the top hemisphere were summarily deep-frozen before they could digest their lunch, and provides an answer to the hitherto unexplained fast rate of melting of the last Ice Age, which has been baffling scientists for some time.

All this gives us an impetus to question and debate our current knowledge with minds open to new concepts. But the important thread which continues throughout the legends of Shining Ones, whether from Mu, Atlantis, Antarctica, another planet, or in most of the old religions, is that they retained what was fundamental to their existence, a direct communication with their creator. The Mystery Schools taught the symbology of the ancients, the true purpose of our life cycle on earth, and the knowledge of ways to communicate with beings of all levels throughout the cosmos.

The Templars were aware of this teaching, and having become the twelfth century equivalent of Thomas Cook, and extremely wealthy to boot, one of their remits was to find evidence of common factors behind the development of the Christian, Jewish and Muslim religions. They believed they might be able to prevent the growth of the already violent schisms which had developed from separate dogma. Perhaps if they had succeeded in their quest, relationships between peoples of many countries would have been very, very different. It was an immense task, with powerful, influential and well-armed mafia-like organisations determined to keep the status quo, so perhaps they can be forgiven for not succeeding. The inevitable happened, and millions of people have since died fighting for ideals and concepts they didn't begin to understand.

Near their Preceptories the Templars have left dowsable evidence of their teaching in the earth surrounding old churches. Strange shapes, spirals, squares, rectangles, crosses, chequer-boards and many other symbols have been recorded by dowsers and confirmed by those with enhanced perceptive talents. Below are illustrations of some of these found around Shipley Church in Sussex.

Some of the energy manifestations found at Shipley

They had a profound knowledge of the effects of sacred geometry on our psyche, and initiated a prodigious programme for the creation of cathedrals and churches in the twelfth and thirteenth centuries. Their understanding of the subtleties of mathematical proportion has been lost for centuries, and we are only now reawakening to a full appreciation of their work. They used an enlightened coordination of earth energies, materials, light, colour, sound and architecture, with an extraordinary range of fine builders and craftsmen in stone, wood, metal and stained glass, managing to complete the most complex constructions in a remarkably short time.

Where they found these skilled people in such numbers, with so much work being carried out simultaneously all over Europe, is a bit of a mystery, but find them they did, and seven hundred years later we are in awe of the exquisite products of their labours. Who can wander round Chartres Cathedral without a feeling that perhaps this was the period when our achievements in this field may have been at their zenith? Louis Charpentier in **The Mysteries of Chartres Cathedral** delves deep into the ancient divine knowledge behind the harmony of this great structure. The site was sacred, used by Pagans and Druids long before the birth of Christ. It is on a major confluence of earth-energy lines, one of which we have traced through Bourges Cathedral and on to Le Puy, in Haute-Loire, where it goes through a wonderful, ancient St Michael church perched on top of a spectacular single crag known as the Needle. There *are* steps up to it, and it's really worth the climb. There is another major energy connection from there to the much-used pilgrim route leading to Santiago de Compostela in Spain.

Back in Cornwall we had already established the field shapes referred to in a previous chapter, and found that as more minds became involved in the Fountain idea, the energy patterns became more complex. While the original glyphs had each lasted many months, the rate of change seemed to increase as interest in the phenomenon grew. I had compared notes on the Cornish energy field with those in Sussex dowsed by Ba, who at that time lived in an area where there had been considerable Templar activity, and who had an opportunity to carry out research into the mysterious energy imprints left by them.

In most cases, the dowsing results in Sussex and Cornwall were remarkably similar. On odd occasions Ba would get a mirror image of the shape I had picked up in Cornwall, and subsequent work has shown that there is a marginal difference between the perceptions of a female and a male dowser. In practically every case where we try to locate the precise position of an energy centre there can be a difference of up to fifteen or twenty inches in our findings. It's been interesting to experiment with surrogate dowsing at these places. I use one rod right-handed, put my left hand on her shoulder, blank out my own dowsing, and work through her mind. Invariably I can then pick up the position where she has put her secret mark. We need to do a lot more work on the significance of this intriguing variation.

We still do not understand the meaning of the constantly changing earth-energy glyphs, but Roger Brown in Australia has recorded a prodigious amount of work on their development in Adelaide, and is undoubtedly a world expert on the subject.

For the record some of the shapes we have been able to measure and define very carefully are sketched below. Perhaps they may trigger some reaction .

There is a parallel, in some ways, with the exquisite art forms being created in fields of growing plants, known popularly as crop circles. It really doesn't matter who makes them, and if they're ordinary humans they must be inspired by the Management. The geometric shapes affect our subtle senses. Their function is to

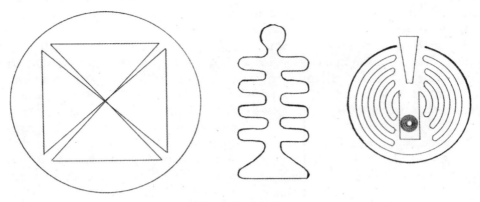

Fountain Glyphs

make us aware of the boundless possibilities in our lives if we would only open our eyes and move beyond the ubiquitous controls which restrict our development. Two comedians, Doug and Dave, were trotted out and paid handsomely to say they had created all these wonderful works, and the thought that the pair of them claimed to have sustained such classic accuracy in the dark, by sighting through a beer-can ring attached to the peak of their baseball caps made me fall about like my little Chinese guide. Of course there were hoaxes, but by no means all of these manifestations were made by sweaty little pranksters with bits of string and lumps of wood on their feet. The media hype had brought things to the stage when questions were going to be asked in very high places about the phenomena, and, by sheer coincidence of course, Doug and Dave just happened along to defuse the situation by ridicule.

No such games with the natural energy forms. They are real, their symbolism recorded through the ages in rock carvings and artwork created by ancient people throughout the world. We are beginning to rediscover their important contribution to our quality of life. With many minds tuning quietly to more caring values, influenced by the gentle energies of the planet, the need for change is becoming an urgent reality. In our current strident society, the standard approach to making yourself heard in the cacophony is either to have a huge advertising budget, for which all of us eventually have to pay, or to shout so loudly and for so long that everything else is pretty well drowned out.

The subtle changes in our minds need no budget and no sound. We know that the energy of earth and universe responds to our thoughts and dreams, particularly to those which are geared to move us out of the self-destructive stasis we are in at the moment. It is only a matter of time before concepts of acceptance, understanding and caring filter through and influence the decision-making process. More than a year has passed since I started on this book, and we now have a different Government in Britain. Not for a moment do I suggest that its members are all whiter than white, but there is a feeling of change in the air which goes far beyond political beliefs. I feel strongly that the caring essence of the global consciousness is beginning to penetrate even the most immovable fixations and we are on the delicate cusp of a new learning curve.

It needs the support of many more people who are aware of the powerful energy of thought to make sure we stay on the upward path.

In the early stages the Fountain network was being run by Trevor and Sheila Nevins, both of whom had a deep understanding of energy-systems. The Fountain ethic flourished under their guiding influence, and many groups were set up to spread the knowledge and practice of the simple healing process.

I spent many a long hour in discussion with Trevor. He was a mystic with a penetrating mind trapped, uncomplaining, in a body which was as restrictive as his mind was free. We dowsed endlessly at houses and sites all over Cornwall and beyond, trying to make some sense of the strange anomalies in energy fields which would appear, change, and lead us on to fresh pastures, with Sheila making intuitive interpretations of the changing events. It was during this period that I learned from Trevor the first steps in working with entities. They are, of course, us, in a different form, and as such have an energy field which can be dowsed. A whole new fascinating vista opened for me, and as he worked with humour, love and not inconsiderable irreverence, undoubtedly he imbued me with the right approach to the subject.

When he died, I was really honoured when Sheila asked me if I would scatter his ashes in a special place on St Michael's Mount where four powerful energies cross. We met in heavy rain on a wild windy morning at Marazion, ready for a soaking on the boat trip across to the island. Sheila was carrying the container with Trevor's ashes in a green Harrods shopping bag and the group smiled with her, knowing that Trevor would appreciate the irony since the store was probably his least favourite establishment. The main scattering of ashes, to comply with the wishes of the authorities, was carried out by the local vicar in the burial ground, and our group moved on to the west of the island to pay our final respects. Sheila had produced another, much smaller container with the real essence of Trevor in it, and Jacob, their son, and I scrambled up to the power centre. It was a simple, moving ceremony at that most important place, and Trevor's approval was tangible.

A few months later I met Sheila in the queue at the local Abbey National counter, and on greeting her I noticed she was carrying the same green Harrods shopping bag. I leaned over and whispered in her ear...

"Who have you got in there this time?"

We both fell to helpless, healing laughter, and could hear Trevor's explosive chortle reverberating with us.

Death is certainly a problem for those left behind, but is a great release for everyone who moves on, particularly to those who have suffered physical pain or distress during their lifetime here. It is part of our learning process, and it's important for us all to accept the absolute truth that while it is the end of one cycle, it is also the joyous beginning of the next.

I *know* this because I've been there.

I had a second visit from Michael Colmer, the clairvoyant who had originally introduced me to the whole concept of earth energy, and as he left I heard him say...

"You'll be giving talks on this stuff shortly."

"Nonsense," I retorted firmly, "I've never given a talk. I don't know nearly enough about anything, even to start, *and this time you are totally wrong.*"

I was quite vehement, and having dismissed it I forgot all about it.

Shortly after that the phone rang, and the organiser for the NFSH chatted about a lack of funds which was affecting the work of a local group.

"I was wondering if you would do a little talk about dowsing to a few people at St Mabyn next month to raise some cash?"

In spite of the strident alarm bells, I listened dumbly, with mounting horror, to hear my voice saying...

"Yes, of course I will. "

I put the phone down, wondering what insanity had prompted me to agree to do it.

It was the eleventh day of the eleventh month, a cold, wet, dreary, misty November night and the St Mabyn Hall was dark, locked, and empty shortly after seven p.m. My spirits began to rise at the possibility that no one, not even the organiser, was going to turn up. Just as I was contemplating a quick escape, she arrived, not in the least put out by the locked door. She departed into the darkness to find help, returning briskly with a slightly surly caretaker who opened the door and disappeared immediately out into the teeming rain calling...

"You have to be out before ten!"

My feeling was that as the meeting was to start at 7.30 we would probably be through by eight. At 7.25 we fidgeted, putting out half a dozen chairs in case anyone might brave the elements, and my executioner said brightly that she thought an author might be coming who knew quite a bit about the subject. It was all I needed to induce complete panic and total memory failure. At 7.29 I suggested that we should retire to the pub for a quick one and call it a night. I was just heaving a great sigh of relief when the door burst open and twenty-two dripping people poured in to the hall ... including the author.

Dry-mouthed I started into unknown territory, trying to find words to convey at least some of my deep-felt enthusiasm for the subject. They were a wonderful, patient, interested audience and I finally surfaced about 10.30 aware of an irate caretaker trying to empty the hall of a chattering group, milling around with coat hangers in their hands, experimenting with techniques of dowsing.

The author was Paul Broadhurst and the meeting had a profound effect on the lives of both of us. We had an animated chat that first evening and he had the grace to come to the second and third talks that 'just sort of happened' in the ensuing weeks. His enthusiasm and knowledge of legend and mystical matters were a spur to delve deeper into related subjects. He had written a splendid book on holy wells called **Secret Shrines**. Now a collector's piece, his depth of research and the quality of his photographs and writing make it a treasured possession in any library.

So when one morning he arrived at the forge with the proposition that we should collaborate on a book, I dropped what I was doing, and we repaired to the Old Quay Pub to sketch out the idea. I had been preparing notes for a book on dowsing and earth-energies for some time but it was still in the dream stage. The input of his expertise and experience with a positive project in mind made all the difference. The inspiration came to him in Merlin's Cave at Tintagel to investigate the 'Michael'

Line, an extraordinary line-up of sacred sites between St Michael's Mount and Avebury in Wiltshire, to see if there was anything significant about the earth-energy system around it.

John Michell, an author and artist of exceptional vision, had perceived this line while contemplating on the Tor at Glastonbury, and as in theory it was a straight alignment, Paul and I reckoned that a few weekends' work might be enough to learn something about it, and possibly produce a small book on our findings.

In the end, of course, it wasn't quite like that. We were immediately introduced to some of the complexities of the earth-energy field, and the story of our four-year pilgrimage was finally published in **The Sun and the Serpent** in 1989. It was an infinitely rewarding time, with sharp, sometimes difficult lessons to learn. Feedback from all over the world and evidence of the profound effect our findings have had on many people's lives served to create in us a deep sense of humility and reverence for the sanctity of our planet.

From the start we had to overcome a number of technical difficulties. We decided to have a few trial runs to develop some sort of modus operandi and see whether we could work together. Paul, quite rightly for his own reputation as a writer, had to be sure that the dowsing results were viable, and I had to be sure that his commitment to the project was more than just the gathering of information to produce another book. It was very quickly established that both of us were deeply involved in the search for a clearer understanding of our relationship with the earth, and there was a mutual feeling that our combined input might produce some interesting results.

I had to be sure that I could find the Michael energy line under any circumstances ... inside the car, outside in teeming rain and wind, cold, tired, under pressure, amongst distracting crowds, clinging to the sides of rocks, or discreetly in a church. I had to be certain that nothing would put me off getting accurate dowsing results.

During some previous research I was following another line to find out whether it connected two important sites in the area. It led me right through Marks and Spencers in Crawley, and three quarters way through the ladies underwear department the store detective caught up with me. He was very polite.

"Excuse me, sir", he said rather tentatively, because my rods are quite big and come to a sharp point. "What are you doing?"

I leaned confidentially over to him.

" Actually, I'm looking for oil."

"Oh!" he said, with some relief, "that's all right then sir," and moved off quite briskly. I've never been quite sure why the answer satisfied him, but I was left to dowse in peace.

Looking for Oil

FIRST FALTERING FOOTSTEPS

The first trial outing Paul and I made was to Chun Quoit, a remote sacred site close to the north coast of the Penwith near Morvah. Neither of us had been there and it seemed a good idea to check out an area of unknown territory, have a look at the energies, perhaps take a few photographs, and see if we could work out a practical way of tackling the Michael Line. As Paul was to be the navigator on the Michael journey, he took over the map, had a quick squint, and marched confidently off from the car park to find the Quoit. I followed for a while across quite tricky terrain with bramble, gorse and the usual granite boulders, until my inherently lazy streak, which requires that my walking has to be the shortest way to get to a destination, got the better of me.

"I think we're going the wrong way," I ventured.

"No we're not," with another look at the map." It's just round this valley."

"It would be really interesting to dowse the direction from here," I said. "After all, this is what we will have to do when we start on the line."

The rods swung very positively up the hill at right angles to the way we had been walking.

"O.K." said Paul, disbelieving, but prepared to humour me in my little game.

We ploughed up the hill, and no one has ever been more relieved than I was when we crested the hill, following the direction of the rods, to find the quoit a hundred yards in front of us. Perhaps that was the moment when Paul really began to believe that our journey was a practical proposition. His faith in dowsing was reinforced a short time later in St Just when I located the direction of 'Gentlemen' when he was in urgent need.

Chun Quoit   RAMON LEHNEN

The second hurdle nearly brought the project to an abrupt finish. We had agreed that the only way we could operate was for him to have exclusive access to the map while I did the driving and dowsing. The first thing I had to learn, and very quickly, was to dowse accurately with one rod. I had tried steering with my knees, while dowsing with both rods, but it led to some hair-raising incidents, the last one involving a police car and two very concerned occupants who looked at us with deep suspicion. It is actually perfectly legal to steer with one hand though ... otherwise how could you make the old-fashioned hand signals?

An interesting dowsing development was that you can pre-programme the rod, or rather your mind, to react when it comes to the line and virtually forget about it in between. At the beginning of the exercise, while I was dowsing continually, I was able to work only for an hour or so before becoming unsure of the results through tiredness. By saving the energy of continuous concentration I was able in the later stages to dowse for five or six hours at a stretch.

The navigator, jealously guarding the map, deliberately disoriented me by asking for 'left and next rights' until I had no idea where I was, with these high Cornish hedges on either side. It meant that I really had to concentrate on the 'signature' of the line to find it. I was very determined to tune in accurately and at each point where I found the energy I stopped the car and checked it by walking along the road to make a positive fix. Paul dutifully marked all the spots on the map.

When we got home everything was a bit quiet. He spread the map out on the table and pointed. We had been expecting a straight line. The dots were all over the place.

"It hasn't worked," he said with some disappointment."You must be a lousy dowser."

Memory of the Chun map-reading stirred a heated response. I knew that the points I found were where we had crossed the line. I had felt the positive signature in each place.

"You must be a lousy navigator," ... a bit acidly. "You've put the marks in the wrong place."

We discussed the results over a soothing dram from the last dregs of a wee bottle I had kept for a very long time for a special occasion. And later in the evening we decided to transfer the points to a map with a different scale.

The jumble of points transformed to a weaving line curving across the map like a serpent.

During the years of 'serpenteering' we learned many lessons about the earth. She had secret moods sometimes, when we felt inadequate to interpret her responses; then, as if to encourage us, she would allow us to see her energy flickering from a rock or plant, leading us on to unravel a little more of the story. We were both going through a slightly 'broke' stage, and we found that we could do an entire day's work on a banana and a Mars bar. It became the ultimate serpenteer's lunch and for a long time after, if we were travelling in a car without a browning banana skin and a crushed Mars wrapper, we felt deprived.

For the first eighteen months we were aware of strange anomalies in the behaviour of the line. We had no idea what they meant, but the strangest one was

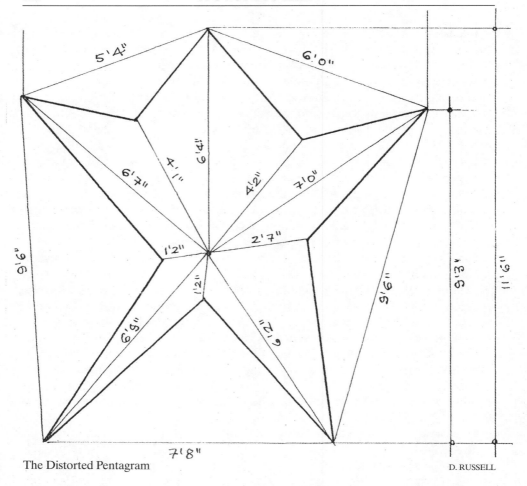

The Distorted Pentagram   D. RUSSELL

that in certain places the energy band, which at that time was about twenty feet wide, came to a point like a pencil, disappeared, and started again a foot or so further on to widen out to its original width. At the point of disappearance we were able to dowse a distinct but distorted version of a five- pointed star.

We were also a bit concerned that the Michael energy seemed to be missing out on quite a few sacred sites which it could easily have passed through. The crucial lesson we learned was that dowsing has to be done strictly honestly, with the information coming from a part of your mind which is not controlled rationally. Had we in any way manipulated the results so that we were happier with what was happening at the time, nothing would have fitted when we eventually discovered the existence of the 'Mary' energy. The strange behaviour of the Michael line was caused by changes in the field induced when the two lines crossed. The same configuration happened with the Mary energy, and these places became known as 'node' points. Mary also visited quite a number of the specially important sites that Michael seemed to have missed. Perversely, if we had been aware of the two energies from the beginning, I doubt very much if I could have coped with the complexity of the dual flow. In the latter stages, working with both, I found retuning from one to the other exhausting, and we settled on the less tiring way of tuning for a morning to the Michael and retracing our steps to spend the afternoon with Mary.

There is no doubt that a prolonged exposure to these powerful energies, particularly at the beautifully balanced nodes, resulted in subtle changes in our perceptions.

When it came to writing the book we had some difficult decisions to make. Our travels had led us gradually into an easy acceptance of happenings which, a few short months previously, would certainly have raised a modicum of disbelief. This was 1988, and there has been a great sea change in thinking over the last ten years.

While we wanted to share all of our experiences, there were some which we knew would strain the credibility of the rest of the story, and reluctantly we decided to keep to matters directly relating to the journey.

We had, with great humility, tried to deal with any discordant energies we came across in a number of places along the line.

At Cadbury Castle in Devon, after dowsing at the side of the enclosure, we both became aware of a strong disturbing tension in spite of the outwardly peaceful beauty of the sunlit trees and green meadow. I had a word with the Management, asking if the line was happy where it was, and was physically shocked by the strength of the almost desperate resounding "No-o-o"... from the universe. Paul and I stood in the middle of the energy and asked if it could be moved to its natural place of balance without harming any life forms. There was an immediate almighty twang like a celestial bowstring, and the energy moved almost fifty feet

The Cadbury Dragon   H. MILLER

towards the centre of the hill. There was a moment of silence, then a susurrus of rustling leaves as all nature seemed to breath a great sigh of collective relief. Focus sharpened as though we had suddenly cleaned our glasses, and we were peacefully and intimately at one with the universe. There are some occasions, if we are really tuned to her energy web, where we can be of help in releasing tensions in the earth's delicate nervous system, which may have built up over generations of misuse or neglect.

Almost a year later I was passing the hill again when I noticed to my consternation that the lovely sculptured tree in the shape of a writhing Cadbury Dragon which we had photographed on our first journey had been blown down in a gale. There she was, her connection with the earth severed, the gasping dragon head wide-eyed, calling for help before the farmer could complete a swift conversion to firewood. There was time to drive to Crediton and buy a saw just as the ironmonger closed. It was almost dark when I returned to perform the delicate surgery of removing her from her binding chains. She was plainly delighted at her release and now sits quietly in a place of honour in my cottage watching events and holding a beautifully contoured alabaster egg from Cyprus in her mouth. I'm not *entirely* sure it hasn't grown a little in the last few months.

Paul and I arrived at Burrow Mump on a November evening, clouds scudding across the sky, now obscuring, now revealing the haunting distant silhouette of Glastonbury Tor. The dowsing had been difficult. It was an important place in the original vision of the alignment, and there was a great pressure to be absolutely sure of the detail of the energy-flow. Perhaps my perceptions had subtly altered because of the degree of concentration, perhaps it was just the right time, or perhaps just plain coincidence, but as soon as we had established the energy line with the node at the original altar, I sensed that the whole of the ruined church was full of people. They had no physical form, but their presence was overwhelmingly strong. I looked at Paul in the gathering darkness and could see by his stillness that he was also aware of them.

"D'you get the feeling that we're not alone?" I whispered.

"There's an awful lot of them," he said quietly.

We were a little subdued that evening, each with our own thoughts on the significance of the experience. We looked forward to further contact with these beings who seemed, by their interested presence, to approve of what we were doing.

It was some months later, at Oliver's Castle, a prehistoric hillfort near Trowbridge on the way to Avebury, when I met them again. It is one of the few places where the straight Michael alignment and the two weaving energies, Michael and Mary, meet at a node point. They form a major pulsing energy centre about fifteen paces to the west of an old dew pond. Ba and I were dowsing the area to verify the energy flow, and while walking slowly towards the pond, we both had the feeling of being watched. There was no one around and, as we worked, our sensitivity to the presences grew. We reached the power centre and sat in the sun, stilling our minds, opening beyond our normal perceptions. Slowly the beings began to take form. They were strolling in groups, talking quietly to each other. From their appearance they seemed to be from many places, from many times, and in all shapes and sizes. They did not seem to mix much, but were courteous and caring with each other, sharing an apparently common source of interest in the fact that someone was working with the energies.

The Watchers

They were not 'visions' but rather 'impressions'. One seemed to be a family group with two very tall thin adults accompanied by two shorter figures who were as interested in the other beings as they were in us. The adults were about eight feet in height and all of them wore identical clothes. It was a dark brown textured collarless coat, buttoned from the waist up to the neck, tied round the middle with a lighter coloured cord or belt, and flowing down almost covering their feet. They each wore a dark, almost clerical hat with a shallow crown and small turned-up brim all round. Their eyes were slightly oriental, very dark and soft. They moved slowly, with great dignity and observed us from some distance as they chatted quietly to each other.

One group was stocky, black haired and bearded, wearing tooled leather clothes with laced gatherings and fringes reminiscent of native Americans, and another was slight, fair, with delicate flowing robes which seemed to disappear at the edges. Whether these were only my interpretations of their energy forms I don't know. Ba was strongly aware of their acknowledgement and support, and found warm reassurance in their involvement in what we were doing. She said she felt like a very special ingredient in a rich celestial cake.

We have met them on many occasions since, usually when working near one of the more powerful centres. Different groups have come and gone, but the tall family in brown clothes always seem to be there, and we have come to welcome them as old friends.

In times of contemplation we think of them as 'The Watchers', the intermediaries between gods and humans, who are aware of our striving to reach beyond our material limitations. At other times, when we are heavily involved in the nitty gritty of this life cycle, we have an irreverent picture of an Angelic Travel Agent selling discounted tickets to time travellers...

> *Your last golden opportunity to observe these primitive five-sensed creatures before they self-destruct. Stunning views of the most beautiful planet in the Universe. Book now before it's too late*

We have come a long way since our first tentative experiments with earth-energy.

We have been through personal traumas, relationship problems, financial pressures, spiritual cleansings, bodily changes almost to a cellular level, accusations of consorting with the devil, and have travelled many a mile of mud-filled roads. We have also had feed-back from many hundreds of people who have been moved to explore the implications behind earth-energy connections for themselves. All of these things have served to fine-tune us to dig deeper into the mysteries of the universe.

Chapter Thirteen

BEYOND THE VEIL

MOST OF US have had an experience at some time in our lives of a happening which can't quite be explained. It could be a flickering movement in peripheral vision so transient that you shake your head and rationalise it as something on your eyelash; perhaps a soft sound of a voice or voices not distinct enough to make out what's being said; or even an object you're sure is not quite in the same position as it was the last time you saw it. Sometimes there's an elusive scent which comes and goes with no apparent source. And, of course, there are the times when you feel that someone or something is in the room there with you.

I had my first experience of this sort of activity when I was about seventeen years old. I had travelled up to the Scottish Highlands to work with my uncle Charlie, who had just established a new timber mill at Carrbridge. I was one of the labourers, lifting the heavy newly-sawn timbers from a gantry, carrying them down the slippery yard and placing them in stacks depending on size and length. The scots pine wasn't so bad, because a little bit of bark was accepted by the customers and allowed for a slightly rounded edge on our shoulders. Larch was different, cut square with an edge that bit into our necks as we slid around, straining to balance while finding the right place to heave the timber off. The sawyers were on piece-work, paid by the amount of stuff they put through the mill, and we labourers were on flat rate, so whenever they threw a belt or stopped to sharpen saws there was a great cheer from us peasants down below. My cousin Ian was a sawyer in another mill and after a few weeks I felt as fit as he looked. He was a tough, sturdy, red-haired Scot with the healthy, ruddy-faced look of someone who worked outdoors all year round in harsh weather.

We played hard too, and one Saturday evening after a wild gale-lashed game of golf and a session at a local hop at Nethybridge we got back late to the house my uncle had just rented till he got established in the area.

Coulnakyle is a typical gaunt, isolated, grey, three-storey highland house in its own area of sparse dark trees, but in its large, somewhat sterile, kitchen we found welcoming glasses of milk and biscuits waiting for us. I still had a warm glow from the feel of the well-built lass in the dark green velvet dress I had danced with, and as I raised my glass ... it was war-time and the rich creamy milk was nectar ... I heard footsteps slowly crossing the floor above the ceiling. I didn't know the geography of the house and I assumed that one of the rest of the family was wandering about. I glanced across at Ian. He was transfixed, glass half-way to his mouth, eyes staring at the ceiling, his usually glowing face the colour of the milk. Wordless, he slammed the glass down and disappeared into the main part of the house. There was no more activity from upstairs, and, intrigued and curious about the whole thing, I went to bed and slept the sleep of the innocent.

The following morning he didn't say much about it except to give me a brief, half-believed story of the mysterious death of a servant girl in the back rooms, at a time when the house was in its hey-day and had a permanent staff in the kitchen quarters. I went into the kitchen, opened a small, unobtrusive door by the side of the range, and crept up the narrow staircase. It led to a couple of attic rooms above the kitchen which had patently never been used for many years. Apart from a few sticks of furniture and some rolls of paper, it was empty. Dust and cobwebs were thick over everything and there was no sign whatsoever of any disturbance on the floor.

The next weekend brought a bright, glorious Sunday morning and the local farmer rang early to see if anyone was available to help get the harvest in. In these days it was quite a usual occurrence in a community which understood the difficult weather conditions, and felt that it was part of the pleasure of living in the country to join in the gathering of the harvest. The tractor and trailer duly arrived and we all piled on to be driven to the field, with the obligatory crate of beer and sandwiches provided by the farmer held firmly by all hands because of the bumpy tracks.

My aunt and her sister were left at home to enjoy the quiet of the day and prepare our evening meal. They had a relaxing day while we worked, and we all felt fulfilled and happy as we sat round the supper table.

"Which of you came back about lunch time for a jersey or something?" my aunt said during a pause in the light conversation.

We looked at each other in mild surprise. It was a long way to the field, and we had hardly stopped all day apart from demolishing the beer and sandwiches.

"No one!"... voices in unison.

"Oh come on", said my aunt, "we were sitting at the window and we heard running footsteps on the gravel outside. The front door burst open, someone ran upstairs, opened and closed a door and came running down again, two steps at a time. We stood up to see who it was ... the front door slammed and no one came out. One of you *must* have been in and somehow crept out at the back for a joke."

None of us had been back, and when we checked the view from the bay window, the whole of the front door and porch could be seen clearly by anyone standing there. And it was impossible to get out of the house in any other way without being seen. Luckily for her peace of mind my aunt didn't believe us, and for a long time afterwards she tried to find out from each one of us separately how we did it. The evening was still and calm but as the temperature dropped after sundown, we lit a log fire in the sitting room. It was a solid house with wide, thick, heavy wooden doors and matching door furniture. We were all fairly soporific after the activities, so when the massive room-door suddenly burst open we were all frozen in disbelief. The two dogs by the fire, a cairn and a scotch terrier like the Black and White whisky advertisement, leapt up and, tough little guys that they are, hurtled towards the door. At the threshold they skidded to a stop, hair rising on their backs, and snarling, both retreated backwards into the room.

My cousins and I grabbed pokers, shovels ... anything to make a weapon and charged through the house, making lots of noise the while to give ourselves courage, torches searching out everywhere. We found nothing, not a window open, not a movement, nothing missing, no one there.

Perhaps it might have been a different story if I had known what I know now, but not long after, my uncle moved the family out to another house nearer Grantown on the pretext that it was a more suitable place for running the business.

I was tickled by the whole thing, and, soon after, came across a book about the Borley Rectory by Harry Price on the investigation of the strange events which occurred in and around it. It was wonderful stuff, but I could find little else at the time that wasn't just an exploitation of some slightly bizarre happenings, and the experience went on the back burner for future reference.

THE OLD FARMHOUSE

In the middle sixties I moved into a fourteenth-century timber framed farmhouse in Sussex. It was in a bit of a state, and I arranged to have some basic alterations done before we actually moved in. I had a builder friend of long standing from up country, and he agreed to come down with his assistant, live in for a couple of weeks, and finish the job. Early in the morning two days later, I met them both coming out of the drive, builder looking grim and the assistant grey-faced.

"We're off to get our caravan so that we don't have to sleep in the house," he said by way of explanation; "Dave here hasn't had a wink of sleep and I feel like a yard of wet string."

I talked to them later and apparently they had decided to sleep in the attic bedroom, the only one not affected by the alterations. On the first night they were awakened by what they thought were subdued voices downstairs and spent the rest of a wakeful night wondering whether they were right. During the second night Dave had been roused from his early slumber by a pressure on his knees and feet, and spent a rigid night waiting for the dawn.

Mind you they were 'townies' and the farmhouse was half a mile from the nearest habitation. Country sounds can be pretty odd sometimes to anyone who is not used to them. I was sleeping in a tent once in an idyllic little glade, with trees all round, when I was wakened by a screech owl. I had never heard one before and I swear my quivering body was three inches off the ground when I came to.

I was excited by their stories and not the least displeased to find later that they managed to complete the work in half the estimated time. Nothing like a bit of subtle pressure to get a job done quickly!

We spent about sixteen years in the house and had a number of experiences which served to stimulate my already growing interest in the subject. One of them was very distressing and had it been repeated it would not have been fair for me to keep my family there. We had moved my young son Sean to a small bedroom on the second floor so that he could have his own space. He was delighted with his room and we had plans to do things which would make it specially his. On the second night we were awakened by a stifled sobbing sound, and when I went in to him he was in a wide-eyed shaking nightmare. He had been through the usual ones that children have, and in each case lying beside him and giving him a cuddle did the trick. This time it was different. His body was rigid and for a long time there was nothing I could do to get close to him. Very gradually the warmth and love got through and he relaxed in deep sleep while I held him until morning. When he awoke he had no memory of what happened and was patently surprised that I was there with him. We moved his stuff into another room and after that he had no more problems of that kind.

Not long after, however, an odd thing occurred in the same room when my stepdaughter brought her young baby down for a visit. It was the Nanny's room over the weekend and, while strolling in the garden outside in the morning sun, she happened to glance up at her window. It was only a few yards away, and inside she saw clearly the figure and smiling face of a Victorian lady holding a small baby. It was so real that she thought someone had dressed the part and was using her charge as a prop! She rushed upstairs to find the baby sound asleep in another room, and of course no one had been near hers. She was an honest, open, well-balanced girl, who had never before had any experience like it, and I believed every word of her description of how she had shaken her head, rubbed her eyes and continued to see the figure for a full ten seconds.

One of the most regular and amusing manifestations we had was the smell of bacon and eggs from the kitchen in the middle of the night. The first couple of times it happened it was so strong that I thought one of the family had got up to have a midnight feast. I confess to an irresistible weakness for the British Breakfast, and both times I got up to join whoever it was in their wickedness. Alas, no such joy. Just a waft to tempt the gastric juices and trigger the thought that now I was up I might as well have some anyway...

In the oak-beamed sitting room there was an inglenook fireplace large enough to sit either side, and it almost became the norm, when passing along the corridor outside, to hear womens' voices, sometimes subdued, sometimes quite vociferous, coming from the other side of the wall. I moved from that lovely house to Cornwall, and regrettably have not had the chance to find out whether the present owners are aware of the other residents.

BACK TO WEST CORNWALL

The move, and the subsequent work on dowsing, very soon brought me in regular touch with many of the strange happenings in this part of the county. The West Penwith, in common with many other Celtic areas, is full of rich legend. Stories of 'spriggans' and fearsome apparitions, piskies and giants abound, and the folklore tells of endless flirting with beings beyond the veil.

I had come back from the tunnel with no fear of these, and in the early days I confess that my motivation to work with them was from a compelling curiosity. I also had a strong feeling of involvement with them, and wanted very much to help, not only the people who were in some sort of distress, but also the beings who seemed to be trapped in their own limbo.

I had heard a great deal about 'black streams', 'black energy', 'negative lines', 'noxious earth streams', 'ley lines', witches' covens, satanic rites and much of the usual paraphernalia of the dark forces. Hushed voices spoke of Crowley, who is reputed to have lived for a short time near St Buryan, and the Terrible Things he got up to. Recent probing reveals no real evidence that he actually did live in the Penwith but the legends and tales of depraved occult practices are still believed by a number of locals. This stuff depends on fear for its energy, and those who want to perpetuate their control by fear are sometimes pretty good at their job.

Once you recognise their way of working, it becomes a lot easier to deal with. It usually starts with someone, male or female, with a bit of charisma who likes to be top dog in a group. You can see it starting in the school playgrounds when the bully gathers a few vulnerable kids around him, telling them he won't thump them if they do as he says. Control through fear has started. It can then be extended through fear of being picked on, ridiculed, or ostracised. Adults in this game usually imply that they have some frightening knowledge of the dark forces which they are willing to pass on to a group of special people chosen to receive it. The fear syndrome is then in place. They arrange meetings with theatrical black candles, dim lights, a few feathers and perhaps a bone or two, and set the scene to produce a group who become too afraid *not* to attend in case something terrible happens.

They can hardly be blamed, really, because we humans like to be frightened sometimes, and willingly spend vast sums of leisure time and money on it. Think of the plethora of films which depend for their success on how long we hide our eyes from the screen, or bungy jumping, or these hairy theme park rides with screaming groups pumping adrenalin and defying gravity in ever more complex fright-machines. The difference with these, of course, is that when they are finished you walk away unharmed, glowing, perhaps, with healthy pride of accomplishment in having got through it.

The other kind of fear sticks, and can become a destructive force in your life.

I took a good long hard look at what was being talked and written about 'black' energy in the light of my discoveries on the nature of earth energy fields. There is no doubt that in some places, and after certain happenings, energy seems to reflect the events and transmit, to anyone sensitive to them, feelings of apprehension, sickness, apathy, depression and foreboding. Equally, of course, it can exude a stimulating, joyous, exciting, all-embracing embodiment of our connection with the universe. The former emotions are automatically associated with the dark forces, and these bring about the debilitating effects of living in artificially-induced fear.

I could not accept the notion of 'evil forces' as a natural part of the delicately balanced earth and cosmic energies with which I had been working since I had my out-of-body contact. Surely if for some good cosmic reason every one of our species was wiped out next Saturday evening, on Sunday morning there would be no Satan, no Hell, no Damnation, no fear of God, no Dark Forces, no Evil. The earth would dust itself off, heave a mighty sigh of relief at having got rid of a potentially lethal skin cancer, and set itself the task of developing a life-form which would care for it a damn sight better than we have.

Dark and evil forces emanate only from our minds, and have no place in the scheme of things, apart from providing one of the means of control in our strange society.

So why do so many people claim that they are being affected by energies which I can't believe are from evil sources? Many other dowsers have published papers or books on the ramifications of energy-fields, but I get uncomfortable with those who seem to find black emanations everywhere, even in their soup. For me the whole of the earth's and the cosmic pulsing grid is composed of benign energies. They have been there for countless millions of years and we have evolved with them and because of them. We are a result of their characteristics rather than being an alien intruder. They cover the surface of the earth and we are exposed to them every moment of our lives. From feng shui, the sophisticated Chinese knowledge of the energy system from thousands of years ago, through the concept of knocking lumps of copper or steel into the earth, to hanging bits of broderie anglaise on spirals of copper wire, experts have pontificated on the efficacy of their particular methods to divert, split, bridge, negate or build the energy flows to their or their customers' satisfaction.

I do not disagree with any of them ... as long as they work.

What I believe very strongly is that the thought process, or the intent, of the mind which is aware of the problem is sufficient to trigger a solution. The method is immaterial and serves only to concentrate the mind. As such, of course, it becomes important to the expert and in fact he may not be able to function without it. What it should never become, by innuendo, word of mouth, ritual or text, is the 'only way to do it'.

I was advised forcibly the other day by an energetic and enthusiastic foreign lady that any results that I happened to get would be improved immeasurably if I scattered blue oatmeal around the area I was working on. My mild suggestion that perhaps this method might not be suitable for me was met by the sort of look normally induced by seeing a worm crawling out of an apple.

By far the greatest number of problems relating to earth-energies come from one simple source. The energies are made up of many different wavelengths and this factor is of crucial importance to our well-being. Each one of us, reduced to our simple elements of life-force, is an amalgam of electromagnetic and biomagnetic energy frequencies, pulsing at continually varying strengths. There are times and places when some of the natural forces of the earth are at odds with those in our bodies. It needs only a minor band to be out of synch with one of ours to initiate a feeling of discomfort. This takes the form of tiredness, depression, or just not feeling one hundred per cent. We are not aware of it, but our bodies begin to compensate automatically for the dissonant feeling and we begin to use our own energy to alleviate the problem. This drain of energy can contribute to the tiredness, increase the depression and, before we know what's happening, we begin to feel really ill. As there are no physical symptoms, it is an impossible problem for medical practitioners, who have enough on their plate servicing our misused bits and pieces; and unfortunately psychiatrists, psychologists, hypnotherapists and the like, with a few very special exceptions, have not yet been exposed to concepts of energy-problems in their respective disciplines.

At first, while I was aware that the issue of energy-resonance was very real, in the light of the increasing number of people who were contacting me for help, I was not sure how to deal with it. Feng shui experts, who were well respected and consequently well paid, had for generations developed ways of deflecting harmful energies by the use of devices called 'mirrors'. They were not mirrors as we understand them but took as many forms as there were experts. The Chinese are natural survivors and astute businessmen, and the deflected energy sometimes tended to be turned towards a neighbour's house, thus providing a potential new customer. Apparently in one area so many were involved that a minor mirror 'war' started with practitioners leaping about furiously adjusting them in vain attempts to outdo their rivals.

Bruce MacManaway was an exponent of using lengths of angle iron for the physical manipulation of the energies and still has a large number of followers. Others use crystals, copper pegs, sheets of aluminium, rolls of wire and even little megaliths built from local stone.

It seemed to me that such an ethereal, natural, although powerful, energy force should not need the application of physical things to influence its being.

It's a bit like pressing flowers with a sledge hammer.

GEO-STRESS AND DISCARNATES

While I was pondering I was asked to have a look at a house in Penzance. The owners were a youngish couple with an early-teenage son, and the husband contacted me because of his concern for his wife's health. She suffered from a perpetual feeling of tiredness and bouts of depression which were affecting their relationship. She had willingly tried every orthodox medical treatment, and complementary medicine had not provided any solutions. The odd thing was that when she went off with the family for a break she was a different woman, with her old sparkle and energy coming back quickly, only to disappear when they got back home. The husband and child were not affected, and while they had every sympathy for her difficulty, they could not understand what was wrong.

With her permission I tuned in to her and then dowsed the house. I found a six-foot-wide line coming through the sitting room, kitchen and bedroom, which included a chord of frequencies with which she must have been very uncomfortable. I sat in the centre of the line, staying tuned to her and became conscious of a pressure in the back of my head between my ears as if someone was stuffing my head to bursting point with cotton wool. My head was singing with discomfort and I explained to her what was happening. I found the direction it was flowing from at the time, and went outside the house to consider how to deal with it. I reckoned that if the frequencies which were causing disruption could be altered to healing pulses, they would not only stop the problem but have the additional merit of actually improving her health. My concern was not only that any change mustn't harm anyone else in the house but any other life form as well. That level of judgement is not in any way available to us, but, having recognised that I couldn't do it, I was aware that I knew some chaps who could. It was equally clear to me they would probably be pretty indifferent to any chunks of arbitrary material I happened to stick on the energy line, so I sat in the middle of it and, as openly and honestly as I could, explained the situation to the Management. The response was immediate, completely simple and logical, and went something like...

"Oops, sorry... of course we can do something about it. We are not aware of these problems in the physical world until someone tells us about them and asks for help."

Not quite in these words, perhaps, but that was the gist.

After a few minutes I went back into the house. The lady of the house was leaning against the door of the sitting room, eyes bright, hand covering her mouth, somehow embarrassed.

"I'm sorry", she said, "I just feel like bursting out laughing."

Her husband, standing beside her with an arm round her shoulder, looked at me.

"I haven't heard her laugh in this house for years", he said quietly.

" Let it go!" I said, grinning at her.

And she did, shoulders shaking, half laughter, half tears of relief. It was a wonderful sound. I left soon after and sat on the wall outside for a moment, perhaps a little misty eyed as I thanked the Management.

"Any time!" came back faintly... and... was that fleeting glimpse of a conspiratorial wink just my imagination?

A week later, a frightened phone call had me gingerly negotiating the rough driveway of an isolated cottage on the moors above Pendeen. Winds are an accepted part of living on this treeless northern side of the Penwith and this night was no exception. Rain glistened on grey granite walls with tiny trees of pennywort sprouting from the cracks. I knocked and could hear bolts and chains slowly drawn. The inside metamorphosed into warm colours reflecting the tastes of the young owner. Some people can transform a house, using the simplest materials and textures, to make a relaxing nest of pure tranquillity. Her body language belied the ambience she had created, and it was with some agitation she described the feelings of desperate despair and deep sorrow which sometimes overwhelmed her. She loved the house, worked unceasingly with her partner to make it the delightful place it seemed to be, but she had now got to the stage where her quality of life was being ruined by the unexplained depressions. She was heartbroken at the possibility of having to leave.

Dowsing located a minor energy anomaly which was easily put right, but I was not happy that this could have had such a profound effect. A deeper probe, ranging into more subtle earth-energies met with no results either, and I was beginning to wonder if there was anything I could do to help. Previous experience gained from working with Trevor prompted me to dowse for the energy-form of any kind of entity. I was hardly prepared for the events of the next few minutes. The reaction was strong and positive, and I was able to pin-point where it was by using the rods in two or three positions and following the direction towards the centre. I put the rods away and approached it, hands a foot or so apart in greeting. When I got close I could feel the energy body as a sort of soft balloon, and was suddenly aware of a deep sense of loneliness, of isolation and a despairing need for communication. My reflex was to pour out love and concern to this desolate being, and the response was immediate. Impressions of who she was flickered through my mind. Gradually it became apparent that she had been a miner's wife around the turn of the century, and was still waiting for her man to come back from the pit. He was long gone, and she had got herself into limbo, half-way between one stage and the next, where it was impossible to go either way. The tentative, unaccustomed communication between us was slow and I was finding it difficult to describe to her where she was, and what effects her presence was having on the physical beings living in the present. The problem was solved by the Helpers, who came in response to my heartfelt call, chattering as usual, apparently totally at home with the broad Cornish accent of almost a century ago. I was aware of them gathering round, supporting, explaining to her where she was, and how their job was to take her with them to the next stage in her life cycle.

They were still chatting eagerly as she disappeared off with them without even saying goodbye. There was a hush in the room. The cottage felt lighter and I could have sworn the ceilings were two inches higher.

Outside the sky had cleared. As I got into the car a shooting star arched in a particularly long-lived streak. I smiled. I didn't really care if it *was* pure coincidence.

At first the calls were mostly from people who began...

'You don't know me, and you will probably think I'm stark, staring, raving mad, but' ... and they would launch into a description of their particular problem. No two cases are ever the same, and I have been constantly intrigued by the diversity of the effects of energy lines and transient life forms.

My experience did not, however, prepare me for an approach by a farmer for some help with his milking herd. The Cornish are of Celtic origin and are well aware of the importance of their close rapport with the earth. There was no embarrassment or holding back in his acceptance that there could be a solution to his dilemma based on knowledge of earth-energies a little deeper than his own. He and his father before him had long experience in handling dairy herds and had always worked to established and tried routines. They had a series of barns with a central walkway along the length and a small step-up on the right and left to individual cowstalls defined by rails. The stalls had the usual feeding troughs fixed to the outer walls and it was a simple, practical system which meant that when the line of cows were munching away, the resulting dung from their rear could easily be cleared along the central lower-level walkway with a scraper in front of the tractor. It was an efficient system until, for some reason, some of the cows started behaving oddly. They would wander down the centre, turn into the stall, stop before they reached the middle, then back round in a 'U' turn into the stall next door. This meant that the eating end was the wrong way and the

Frenzied Friesians

backend to the feeding trough! Consternation all round, with cows bellowing for food one end and doing unspeakable things in the troughs at the other.

Thus it was, one fine evening, I donned wellington boots and went to have a look. The herd had just come in from the field and the farmer and I opened the gate to get in amongst them. They had patiently waited all day, apparently holding themselves in until they got into the yard, and had produced a prodigious sluicing of slurry. I had a quick wonder what on earth I was doing pushing through fifty-odd tonnes of frisky Friesians, all excitedly curious to know why I was marching about with a dowsing rod in my hand, rather than resting at home by the fire with a good book. Cows are funny animals. When you look at them from above, believe it or not, they are slimly triangular, with the head at the pointed end. It enables them to wedge themselves into a solid mighty phalanx of meat which takes a bit of shifting even using the rod as a prod. They finally let us through and we managed to keep them at bay while we had a look at their barn.

I found myself tuning in to the animals. They're really quite endearing close up and I tried to get into their heads. I walked down the centre of the shed and turned into a stall which was obviously one of the problem areas. Half-way to the trough I got a strong reaction which stopped me in my tracks. I tried again, retuning as far as I was able to the waiting cows. Again the same reaction. Running down the full length of the stalls, and half-way along them, was an energy line, only a couple of feet wide, but which included a frequency or series of frequencies which some of the animals didn't like. It was enough to stop them and they had learned quickly that if they reversed in they didn't feel a thing. The Ministry of Agriculture experts had scratched their heads and blamed everything, including the height of the restraining rails, without coming up with an answer. A quick word with the Management confirmed that they were just as concerned with the wellbeing of the animals as they would have been with humans, and the energy frequencies were subtly changed to solve the problem.

It was too much to expect an immediate result, because cows are creatures of habit and have to be persuaded to unlearn things, but I gather that the farmer has reverted to the time honoured way of shifting the slurry from the barn. Official explanation? Just a coincidental change in the cows' behaviour... of course.

I have spent many an evening trying to alleviate stresses caused by rogue energies, and as a result came across entities of many shapes, sizes and ages, from recent times to centuries ago. Most couldn't wait to go; some were reluctant to leave what their restricted senses had come to believe was a tolerable billet, clinging to their earth-experience; and some had been in limbo so long that it needed a benevolent visual severing of roots that were almost physically holding them to the earth. I began to think I was getting the hang of how to help them.

THE RELUCTANT MONK

So when I got the call from a dear old lady who lived in one of the prettiest little villages in south Cornwall, I was delighted to go over one Sunday in June. I looked forward to seeing the place again at this lovely time before it became packed by tourists, and anticipated a routine meeting with whatever was causing the problem. She was hesitant at first to explain what was wrong, because she was quietly devoted to the delightful little church just round the corner and didn't want to cause any upset. I assured her that whatever I did would be with absolute discretion and that no one else would be in the least aware that anything out of the ordinary was happening. It seemed that a number of people in the congregation had been disturbed by the appearance in the church at odd times of the shadowy figure of a monk. He was always very quiet and peaceful but some of them had become afraid to go into the building except during the service. The local vicar was inclined, for some reason, to laugh it off, and she was very concerned to find someone who could help. In the afternoon, after the service, I dowsed round the church picking up the lively energy line marked by an exquisite old standing-stone just outside the walls. Inside it was a peaceful haven, oak pews polished with age, uncomfortable as ever, making sure you suffered as you sat and didn't sleep during the sermon, colour and light dancing from movement of leaves through stained glass. My eyes adjusted from the bright sunlight and I was aware of something at the far end of one of the pews on the right side of the church. I slid quietly into the seat and, slowly, as if recognising that I knew he was there, a figure began to take form beside me. He wore a brown monk's habit with a hood and his head was bowed forward in his hands. I thought he was in prayer and waited a while. He was holding something cupped in his fingers and I finally recognised it as a honeysuckle blossom. He had a benign, gentle old face and as he raised his nose from the flower he was plainly curious as to why I had approached him. I found myself explaining the dilemma of the people who were afraid to come in to the church, and asking him if he needed any help to move on to a more congenial place.

He was contrite. He told me modestly that he was a fairly advanced spirit who was free to revisit places he had loved on earth for pure nostalgic joy and the beauty of natural growing things in our dimension. He was in distress that his presence had intruded on the senses of some of the congregation and apologised for indulging his own pleasure to the extent that he had encroached beyond his normal boundaries. I was numb with embarrassment for the gaucheness of my approach, and he smiled in sympathy.

"It won't happen again," he seemed to say, "but I shall still come back whenever I need."

He took a deep long sniff of the flower and, smiling in blissful appreciation, faded silently away.

I went back to tell my story to the old lady, and she listened with eyes bright with understanding, nodding at the end of it. On the way home I reflected on the afternoon. I had been introduced to something wonderful ... a confirmation of continuity and free-will in the universe. I felt chastened, very small, and desperate to share it with everyone I could.

Some months later I went back to the church. It was still as beautiful as I remembered and welcomed me as I opened the door. I slid into the same pew, meditating on the now fond memory of the old man. He wasn't there, of course. As I turned to go something stopped me, and I looked about to find out what it was. A faint waft of honeysuckle wrinkled my nose.

In November?

It became clear after working for some time with 'discarnates', as many people call them, that they are just one of us in a different form. Almost invariably they are lonely, sad, and desperate to make some sort of contact with

The Reluctant Monk

us, because they are trapped in a limbo where there is no communication either way. The fact that they manage to manifest somehow into our range of senses is a measure of their need for contact. They usually are aware of the most sensitive person around them, and apply bursts of energy to convey their presence in a lonely cry for help. The result can be in the movement of small objects as with a 'poltergeist', or with physical pressure on our limbs, a fleeting visual manifestation, a smell, or sounds. The object is to bring themselves to *someone's* attention so that they might be able to get some assistance.

Unfortunately they are usually met with fear, or, from some religious sources, a total lack of understanding and a threat of banishment. I shall never understand why an accidentally-drowned seaman who manifested in his oilskins to the crew of a fishing boat could be treated by an exorcist member of the clergy as a representative of the devil. This was a recent occurrence and smacks of a mediaeval witch-hunt. The Management tell me they can't reach across the veil, and they need someone on our side to intercede so that the spirit can move on of its own free will. Some of them don't realise that they are no longer tied to the earth. It happens a lot with sudden accidents where there is a tendency to cling on to the familiar aspects of living. In some cases the feeling lasts so long that the knowledge of how to go on is obscured and forgotten. What is absolutely essential is that each and every one of them must be treated with respect, love and understanding, and their present situation must be carefully explained to them so that they can make positive decisions about moving on to the next stage. People who appear to be 'possessed' often have a small, frightened entity clinging to them for security. The host sometimes develops a feeling of protection for the entity, rather like caring for a newly-found kitten, and it requires a great deal of time and energy to get a clear understanding of the situation through to both of them, to unravel their mutual dependence. There is often a great deal of primitive fear involved which must be overcome before a start is made to solve the problem.

By no means all 'bumps in the night', mysterious bell-ringings, swinging chandeliers, clinking glasses, and doors that fly open are attributable to frustrated entities crying out for our attention. In a recent paper to the Society for Psychical Research, and later to the BSD Earth Energies Group, Anne Silk, an accomplished seismologist and lateral thinker, gave chapter and verse on the practical reasons behind many of these phenomena. Resonant effects from distant earthquakes, earth movements and faulting, can produce vibrational frequencies which can not only make things wobble, but also stimulate micro-magnetic fields in our brains which make us think we are seeing, hearing, smelling, tasting or touching something. So when a strange happening comes up for investigation it's as well to assume at first that there are perfectly rational natural explanations for it.

But I don't think such resonant frequencies would have conjured up the old monk with his nose in the honeysuckle.

Sooner or later you're liable to come up against the downside of energy work. In the early days Ba and I were urgently moved to visit the scene of the Brixton riots in South London the morning after the news broke. We hoped to be able to help with some positive input to that deprived, unsettled area. There were still signs of the disturbance as we dowsed for energy manifestations which might give us a clue on how to assist, and which would be the best place to apply healing energy. On a wide pavement we found a shape which had us both clutching at our solar plexus in a reaction which seemed to drag us down into a grey, murky pool of desolation. It showed us the seriousness of the situation. Similar shapes, but of course much stronger, had been dowsed before, and still persist around the sites of some of the concentration camps in Germany. The ambience goes beyond realms of depravity towards a feeling of dehumanisation. In Brixton at that time things were beginning to head that way.

We were shocked by the discovery and tried, with the little knowledge we had, to help in any way we could. We felt woefully inadequate in the face of the strength of the manifestation, and were quietly reflective and subdued on the way back to Sussex. We had arranged to go to a Yoga class in the afternoon run by Kate and Jack Money in Worthing, and I went off to Lancing Chapel to lick my wounds, meditate, and look for any sort of guidance. The huge chapel was lit from behind the altar, and empty when I walked slowly in. I stood in the centre of the aisle looking at the great tapestry on the wall at the back, responding to a first realisation that the design incorporated a large fountain.

I watched for some time and finally voiced my feeling of inadequacy.

"What on earth can I do about anything as vast as what went on at Brixton?"

Nothing happened for long moments then a little voice inside started to tell me to go home and forget the whole idea. It was all too big and, anyway, none of my business. I was reluctant to accept that there was *nothing* I could do, however small, and suddenly became aware that I was finding it difficult to focus on the tapestry. I rubbed my eyes, shook my head, and looked again. The fuzziness stayed. There seemed to be writhing movements within it, and at the same time I heard what sounded like the soft rushing of wind through branches coming from behind me. The sound increased as the tapestry came alive and I received an almost physical blow on my shoulders and the back of my head. I ducked down involuntarily and looked again behind the altar. All was still, silent, and I began to think that tiredness had perhaps induced a slight fainting fit although I had never experienced such a thing before.

A message came through, loud and strong ...

"This is just an inkling of the energy that is available to all of you when you are capable of handling it."

Outside, I felt replenished, refreshed and full of energy, certainly with some misgivings about being such a weak-kneed wimp on the Brixton affair, but with a new enthusiasm which has stayed with me ever since.

THE ROAD TO THE ISLES

Kate, in her wisdom, had decided that the afternoon yoga session would concentrate on shoulders and neck. I spent the time gently getting rid of what felt like quite a severe sunburn on the top of my shoulders. It was actually two or three weeks before the effects completely disappeared. Many years later I told Kate the story. She just grinned and said she had got the message on what part to work on about lunch-time. She and Jack became great friends of ours and were a massive support to Ba and me during difficult times. They went off for a brief holiday in Skye, fell in love with the island, and bought a superb old granite hunting-lodge on the edge of the sea. They wanted to have it as a retreat centre and somehow managed to complete the deal in the space of a few days. Tragically Jack died very suddenly before they could move up there. When he was near the end, I sat with him for a while. He was very weak and was not capable of talking, but he gripped my hand very fiercely for a long time. I knew that he wanted us to help Kate realise the dream of Skye after he had gone. He and I went part way on the journey towards the tunnel, and as I left him to complete his pilgrimage I knew that he would be with us to help bring the dream to reality.

Quiraing Lodge   H. MILLER

Ba moved up to Skye to supervise the rebuilding and refurbishing of the lodge ... and to make some major decisions about her own life ... until Kate was ready to take over. She spent a purifying year there, plunging into the local life, cutting and carrying peat, and handling the complexities of builders and gale-torn disappearing roofs with equal composure. During that time Kate asked me if I would drive up to Skye with a lorry full of furniture and bits and pieces she had collected for the lodge. I was delighted to help and spent an evening packing the largest version of a Transit van so enthusiastically and innocently that another postcard would have bent if I had forced it in. It was dark and late when I'd finished.

Starting long before dawn I was vaguely aware that the vehicle was hunkering down a bit at the back, but there was a long way to go and not much time to do the journey. Somewhere north of Birmingham I was singing loudly when I saw the blue flashing lights. Coming abreast with window down, the policeman motioned for me to follow him and we diverted down a track to a weighbridge.

"What've you got in there?" he said politely

"Only a few sticks of second-hand furniture and household stuff." I replied, equally pleasantly.

"The system is," he said, "we weigh the front axle first, then the back one, add 'em both together, and see if you're over-weight. If you are, either you stop here, or you chuck off your load until you're legal. Your own risk, of course ... up to you."

My heart sank as he looked at the back axle with a knowing shake of his head. What on earth in this precious collection could I abandon to save the rest?

The two constables retired to a little shed and beckoned me on to get the front axle in place. They checked it, nodded, and I started forward to get the back wheels onto the machine. I looked skywards for inspiration and saw, wheeling around, (just north of Birmingham... remember?) a lone seagull. Jack had often said he'd love to come back as one to soar over the Skye sea and cliffs, and I called out...

"*Jack!* We have a problem!"

The back end of the truck seemed to lift when we got on the weighbridge. The two policemen looked, and looked again in disbelief. Three times they made me drive on and off the thing, each time conferring and shaking heads. One of them finally came out, quizzical eyebrows raised. These fellows really do know their stuff and normally don't waste people's time unnecessarily.

"I've given you a certificate," he said, still doubtful and looking inside the vehicle.

"You're less than a kilogram under weight, and you can show this ticket to anyone else who stops you."

My cheery wave of goodbye left them still not convinced.

"Thanks, Jack." I breathed, pulling out on the motorway. "Thanks a lot!"

When Ba finally joined me in Cornwall after her long stay in Skye, I took her to the top of my beloved, wild, remote Trencrom Hill to show her the stunning view. She looked for a while, taking in the sea on both sides, the distant shore lines, St Michael's Mount in the bay, the granite and gorse, the rolling countryside and said...

"My God, isn't it crowded!"

She added another dimension to my work on energies. With her intuition and experience she could pick up things which I had missed or failed to register, and we continued on investigative forays into the strange effects that came our way. She became widely experienced in dealing with energies liable to cause any kind of discomfort, and our combined sensitivities covered a much broader spectrum than before.

On one occasion we were asked by a distraught lady for some help in her house on the Isles of Scilly. She ran a Bed and Breakfast, and was dependent on the income for survival. Apparently there was a problem with one room in the house where guests were extremely unhappy, and some had left before the end of their week's holiday. It was extremely worrying for her, and a bizarre series of accidents to other guests, one of which was serious, had brought her to an almost suicidal state.

We flew over as soon as we could to see her. She greeted us tearfully, and filled us in with the details of an astonishing sequence of disasters as we drove to the house. Outside the house we checked from two directions, locating a strong energy form somewhere inside. We were led to a little bedroom upstairs, which we learned later was the one with the problem, and felt a malevolent, disruptive air when we entered. It was hardly necessary to use rods to find the energy source. When we approached, the entity responded with anger, not particularly at us, but rather at the world about it. Slowly we established communication, and learned that he had moved from another part of the island where a previous life-style had been extremely unhappy. It took a long time to get any sort of message through, but gradually there was a release of the pent-up fury, and it became possible to bring in the Helpers to cope with the difficult guidance.

When the final moment of parting came, Ba and the owner were leaning back against the wall of the bedroom. They both felt the wall shake and vibrate and heard a thump from downstairs. It was some hours later that the altered energy-field rebalanced, the repercussions rippling on and slowly disappearing. We were having a cup of tea in the sitting room when the owner noticed that the glass in front of the unlit wood burning stove had cracked and fallen out. She had replaced it a couple of days before so it must have gone when the wall shook. We checked again all round and while I was happy that the entity had gone on its way, Ba had reservations which she couldn't quite pin down. We discussed it during the evening but couldn't get to the reasons behind it. That night it became clear. She was awakened suddenly from a nightmarish dream which could only have been a psychic attack triggered by the raw, residual malice left by the entity before departing. The visual image was extremely unpleasant and, acutely aware that if she was to continue with this sort of work she would have to deal with it herself, she immediately challenged the attack. The energy form dissipated and vanished, but the memory of it is still there. It was a cauterising lesson for her, and she was spiritually immeasurably stronger after the experience.

Some years before, I had gone through a similar experience of attack, although this one did not attempt to create fear. It had been a very difficult fortnight, with a number of things going wrong which required a great deal of effort to put right. I was due to meet Paul to finish an important part of the dowsing up-country and time was getting short. We had a really tight schedule ahead when I left home in the little diesel-engined Golf which had served us so well on our journeys. It was the Friday before a Bank Holiday, and I was in a rush to get off before the real traffic started. There seemed to be a huge load in the car, thrown inside in a heap before leaving. Black clouds ahead promised some fierce rain. A few miles along the dual carriageway I pulled out to pass a car and accelerated. I was just past, and preparing to move into the inside lane when I felt the car moving faster. The engine speed increased well beyond normal and I braked to compensate. No effect at all. As the whine of the engine changed to a shriek and black smoke started to fill the car, I switched off the ignition and knocked it out of gear. I discovered then that diesels don't worry about things like ignition, and the shriek reached the pain threshold. By this time the black smoke had filled the car, reaching my lungs, and I couldn't see a thing. Spluttering, I groped for the bonnet catch and snatched on it, rolled out the door, and, heaving the bonnet open, finally tore off the fuel feed pipe to the engine. She gave a final scream and stopped suddenly. All the savings from the low fuel consumption for the last three years, and a lot more, went up with the black smoke. The engine was a hot, crackling, twisted write-off. Slamming the door, I set off, sprinting along the dual carriageway to find a telephone box. The heavens opened a few minutes later, and, having left my jacket in the car, I was drenched by the coldest rain I've ever come across in Cornwall. The nearest telephone box was out of order and when I got to the next one I found I had no change. Eventually, after nightmarish delays, I got through to the friend who usually fixed the car, and he said he would pick me up and tow me back. I started back to the car, exhausted, soaked and shivering, sick at the thought of the ruined engine and the impossibility of accomplishing all we had carefully planned for the next few days. As I splashed along the side of the road I think I was at my lowest ebb when I came to a bridge with a tubular handrail. Looking down through the driving rain I could see a road winding along about a hundred and fifty feet below. I stopped for a moment, weary of the whole thing, and became aware of a soft but insistent voice inside my head...

"Go on!" it said persuasively. "You're an advanced being. You can fly. Go on. Try it!" and I could almost feel it helping me over the rail.

There was a brief moment before I realised what was happening, then a huge anger at this invasion provided energy for the response. I confess to using a colourful collage of four letter words and images derived from my time in the army, and was gratified at the immediate effect. Making use of the old ceremonial ways I quietly reflected back the thought patterns to whoever had initiated them. After all, if they make that sort of decision, which they are perfectly entitled to do, they have to accept the responsibility for the results of the decision. My friend arrived a few minutes later, and his lady, bless her, having rung around for a replacement car, drove me to pick it up. Within half an hour I was on my way again, dry, and with my faith in the order of things fully restored. It was a very successful trip, as often transpires when something catastrophic happens right at the beginning, but the memory of the insidious attack remains with me as a constant reminder of the possible pitfalls that may be encountered when you are involved in the investigation of energies.

THE "BLACK MICK"

I certainly needed Ba's supportive strength on the occasion when I had my most profound experience of people who try to manipulate by using malevolent forces. I had been asked to have a look at a site near Primrose Hill, north of Regent's Park in London, which seemed to be getting more than its fair share of misfortune and bad luck with illness, accidents, and the breakup of relationships. Mike Colmer had initiated the probe because of a series of odd happenings to a number of his friends in the area, and, because he had first introduced me to the energy conundrum, I felt pleased that I might be able to do something in return. I dowsed and picked up something I had never experienced before. There was an energy-band encompassing brooding frequencies in a minor key, which I found not only uncomfortable, but which also induced a deep sense of foreboding. I followed the line through a number of streets and crescents, noting the various buildings it went through, and was disturbed to find that the strong centre part of it was nearly twenty paces wide. I had no time to do more during that visit, but felt some disquiet as I pushed a note through Mike's door. I remember the content clearly. I gave details of the houses affected and ended with a quick note. "It's not a local thing, Mike. It's a big hefty black about twenty yards wide and I'll have to have a look to see where it comes from and where it's heading."

I had no idea what I was letting myself in for.

A few months later I was becoming increasingly concerned about the nature of the line. I had followed it across country to the north west, and picked it up very close to Chequers and one of the combined Army, Navy and Airforce headquarters close by. Further on it went just north of Chipping Norton, through Evesham, over the notorious Meon Hill, site of a ritual murder, and smack through the middle of Worcester and Hereford County Hall. From there it passed just south of Ludlow and Bishop's Castle leaving the Welsh coast on the point at Barmouth west of Dolgellau. A map projection put it through Dublin but I had no chance to dowse over there to confirm its position. In the other direction, the line took in many influential buildings in the city before passing through Wapping, the scene of Murdoch's first real power struggle, then just north of Maidstone and Ashford before crossing the coast at Folkestone.

I suppose the most disturbing factor was that it pulsed at continually varying strengths, indicating that it was being actively used. I had no idea for what purpose, except that I was getting clearer and more insistent messages from the Management that all was not well, and that the energy was being used by someone for very much the wrong reasons. I began to get confirmations from other sources that this was the case, and the little bits of information added to a determination to see what could be done. I wanted to know where it was coming from and did some rough extensions on the map, which showed that the feed could emanate from Iran. Some expert map dowsers confirmed that they could pick it up going through Semiram and Abadeh, about a hundred and fifty kilometres south of Esfahan. I was pondering how to find out more about this area when into the forge walked a friend of mine, Joe Bendle, a mine surveyor. Yes, he had worked there, and yes, he had maps of the area, and yes, he had some local knowledge of what went on in that part of Iran. He told me of the strange ancient city of Bam, whose buildings look as though they are still habitable, and which was well established at the time of Alexander the Great. While he was there no local Arab would enter the city, in spite of the poverty in the area. It was known as a 'bad place' with a legendary curse on it that struck fear into the bravest, from its association with the hashshashin or hashish-eaters, a term originally referring to members of an Ismaili sect who took the drug before attacking their enemies, and from whom the name assassin was derived. The line appeared to go as far as Bam with no trace beyond. I checked it regularly and found that the strength seemed to be increasing sporadically. Certainly there was a lot more activity within the line than there had been when I first found it in the area of Regent's Park.

I thought it would be prudent to ask an established religious exorcist for advice and perhaps some cooperation in handling what was rapidly becoming a major foray into the world of the darker forces. Initially he was at pains to persuade me not to be involved under any circumstances, since my experience and training had not been channelled through the church. When he realised that I was going ahead with it anyway, he spent some time giving details of satanic practices obviously calculated to frighten me off. I was intrigued by this deliberate attempt to induce fear, and it was only when I related my experience in the tunnel that he relented and made some positive suggestions on some of the methods used by the church in these circumstances. He did admit further that grapevine whispers told of satanist groups who had been trying to build energy for some time in preparation for a major event. I left with a rather battered copy of the English Hymnal which includes an invocation for protection 'Against all Satan's spells and wiles ... and wizard's evil craft."

Advice from people who had played a part in negating harmful practices varied enormously in detail, and was sometimes conflicting, but a number of things became very clear as I progressed. One was that at the moment of confrontation I had to be in a state of grace, the second that I had to declare that I was there of my own free will, and the third that everyone involved had to use pure, unconditional love to reduce the effects of the corrupted energies.

The object was to alter the harmful frequencies so that they could no longer be used for manipulation, and to ask that the energy should be replaced by those which would respond to love, care and healing. I drew the line on a map and worked out a triangulation system which incorporated energy from the St Michael Line, St Michael's Mount, Lancing, Royston, Evesham, Stafford and London. It clearly defined the position I should take up, on the A421 a couple of miles south of Bicester. The timing was set for six-thirty in the evening before the solstice, the date of the powerful event that the exorcist had linked with the satanists. I had Ba in the hot seat holding the top of the triangle, and a trusted friend at each of the relevant crossing points. At about six o'clock I arrived near the point where the line came out from a field and crossed over a minor road. I dowsed quietly to discover the exact position of the centre of the now fiercely strong line, and marked it with a stone. In the direction of the flow right in front of me was a thick, six-foot high hawthorn hedge.

By six twenty-five my heartbeat must have been close to 160, but two minutes before the half-hour it started to quieten down to normal. I had been meditating with my friends at the end of the tunnel, and the Management had given me a lot of support for the enterprise. Walking into the centre of the line was still a considerable effort, and as I turned to face the direction of the energy flow, I declared aloud that I was there of my own free will. I called on the forces of creation to transmute the raw energy of fear to a benign healing level and immediately my perceptions changed to a point about four feet above my head. I could 'see' over the hedge in front of me and down from what seemed an extraordinary height to the ground in front of me with incredible clarity. I had an impression of standing in front of a great, black, onrushing express train which enveloped me, and which seemed to have endless power in its thrust to get past and annihilate me. I was also aware of the strength of support in the shape of sparkling, crackling energy around my body. It seemed to take two or three minutes of intense concentration before the fury gradually abated. As my perceptions began to revert to normal I could almost hear the message...

"All right ... we've got it now!"

... and I could feel the altered energy coursing back down the line through the Michael connection, on through London, burning back through Folkestone and Europe and finally to Iran. It was ten minutes before I moved out of the line. I felt completely drained, and it seemed to take forever to cover the fifty yards to the car. I sat motionless for a long time, trying to assimilate the incredible importance of what had just happened. It was a salutary lesson on the amount of power which can, in special circumstances, be generated through fear to influence other people. I still had an uncomfortable feeling that, although the whole operation had been successful beyond measure, I couldn't relax until I was some distance away from the scene. I started the car and drove much too fast along the road which would get me back to Ba. From somewhere deep inside I had a 'Tam o'Shanter' reaction which made it urgent to put water between me and the depravity which I had sensed from the black energy of the express train. I shot over a bridge and felt what seemed like the comforting thump of a solid security door closing behind me. Only then did I relax and drive the car more sedately into the night.

Ba saw my depletion and tears of exhaustion and was able, by using the earth's natural frequencies and her own healing talents, to build and recharge me within a few days. She, along with everyone who had been involved, was sombrely aware of the savage forces which had been applied to preserve the line by the people who found it useful for their own dubious purposes.

Since this time we have regularly checked the line, now irreverently referred to as the "Black Mick" because it was the antithesis of the St Michael Line, and it is still benign and healing.

If nothing else happened, I'm willing to bet that the quality of life in Worcester and Hereford County Hall is a bit better than it used to be.

HUMILITY

We meet an increasing number of people, many of whom have spent no more than a couple of hours with a pendulum at a dowsing seminar, marching around sacred sites declaring...

"The energies were in an awful state ... but it's all right - we've balanced it and it's all O.K. now."

Their intent is fine and certainly they cannot do a lot of harm to energies which have been going about their business for a few million years. What really happens is that their own energy fields are influenced by the site. They feel the benefit of the new balance and attribute it to their 'sorting out' of the earth. She is incredibly generous and patient with us and smoothes our jagged chakras to prevent us disturbing her like little buzzing flies.

I cannot stress enough the importance of humility and care in this work.

Indigenous people around the world, who have hundreds of years of history of communicating with the earth, are coming to terms with itinerant do-gooders who drop in to 'fix things'. Places like Ulhuru in central Australia have a bit of a problem at the moment because it's the 'in' place to sort the energies out. No doubt the fashion will move on. No one who is not delicately tuned to the culture of the indigenous people and the subtle whispering earth energies can hope to perform anything other than a superficial rite at these sacred places.

This is not in any way to denigrate the efforts of many hundreds of sincere and dedicated people who have reached a level of perception which allows them to work with the energies for the common good. A surprising number around the globe spend a great deal of their time and effort in implementing and teaching the many ways to tune in, and I have a spine-tingling feeling that their message is beginning to break through. Even if it's just placing a crystal, with the right intent, in a holy well, it helps build the connection of being at one with the elements. It's a purifying process which can lead us to a major shift in values.

It was an eye-opener for us when we visited Russia to find that our exploits here are only on the very outer fringes of work on the 'paranormal'. We spent a lot of time with a Professor Alexander Neklessa, chairman of an Institute of the Paranormal in Moscow, which had been functioning for over thirty years. One of their remits was the exciting and far-seeing concept of regressing suitable people to some of the legendary ancient civilisations in order to find out about their culture, and, if the society failed, to discover what went wrong with it. Social and political decline was to be of greater interest than destruction by natural catastrophe, and the idea was to design from the results a new culture which might not be as susceptible to failure as the old ones. We were astonished, of course, because the whole idea implied a private acceptance that at some future date the communist ideal would inevitably fail, and that work on defining an alternative was being given some priority. They always worked with a combination of scientists and mystics, each having the same status, so that scientists were helped to apply their minds to problems outside their own discipline, and mystics had to assume a critical responsibility for their work.

The results from the sessions involving Atlantis were particularly interesting. Over a number of years many pairs were given an exercise to carry out a controlled regression to the ancient legendary city. The physical description of the place was fairly consistent throughout, but reports of the culture and social organisation of the city were found to be split into three distinct categories. One was of a completely female-dominated society, with male intellectuals and thinkers making major contributions to social development, but not being allowed to take part in any of the control or organisation. The second, quite the reverse, was a male-dominated authority, with females treated with respect, but not being allowed to take part in the decision-making process. The third was a balanced male/female life-style where equality was paramount, and there was no concept of one sex having greater rights and degrees of authority than the other. The differences were astonishingly detailed and each pair was checked and rechecked on the accuracy of reporting.

An interesting point was that the three-way split on the different interpretations was almost evenly balanced. The Institute felt that the evidence was strong enough to support the conclusion that in Atlantis there must have been three parallel realities in existence at the same time.

It's a pretty profound inference, and the professor postulated the theory that if this was the case, perhaps in our own time we are also living in one reality while others exist in parallel. He again arranged for scientists and mystics to probe this possibility, and after some experiments with what appeared to be a form of time-shift, a number of the mystics came back with reports of reaching what appeared to be a high wall of grey mist. Some of them agreed to try to penetrate this to find out what was on the other side, and within a short time came back with stories of another race, slightly taller than us, but in another parallel reality in which there seemed to be a great deal of dissatisfaction and dissent. The professor stopped the experiment, not because he was afraid of what he might find, but because the mystics began to find it difficult to cope back here with the knowledge that another race could be living in parallel time with us but in a slightly different dimension. They began to show signs of serious distress and he felt that he didn't have the right to ask them to continue with work which might have affected their balance, or even their sanity.

Perhaps when our perceptions have reached a higher plateau we will be able to handle these and other higher concepts with equanimity and understanding, but I think we still have a long way to go before our minds can accept our real place in the universe.

Chapter Fourteen

COSMIC CONNECTIONS

A GROUP OF fishermen were rowing back across the bay to St Michael's Mount one night in the fifth century when one of them glanced over his shoulder to check whether they were on course for the small harbour. His hoarse frightened cry alerted the others and all looked in the direction of his pointing finger. On the right-hand side of the island near the top a bright source of light had appeared. They gazed spellbound, seeing movement within it forming and reforming, convinced it was a manifestation of the Archangel St Michael appearing to confront them with their sins. They were all respected men in the community and their story was believed, recorded, and probably much enhanced in the telling. Some considerable time later the apparent position of the apparition was marked by a small standing stone near the edge of a cliff on the west side of the island.

I believe them completely.

Not the bit about it being St Michael, because given the fearful superstitions of the time it was probably a perfectly logical interpretation of the strange

Apparition at the Mount

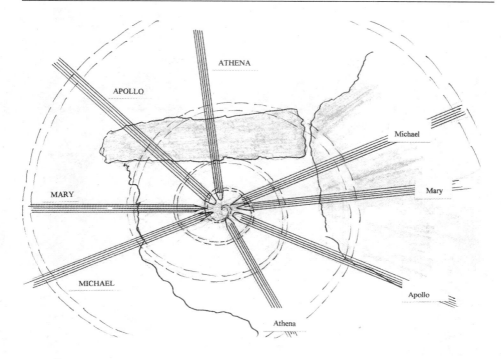

Cosmic Connections

phenomenon, but the story of the appearance of the light source itself. Nowadays it would be the centre of an excited media probe into an unidentified flying object account and doubtless would trigger frightening implications about what the aliens would do to us when they arrived.

When Paul and I worked on the island during the research on **The Sun and the Serpent** we found a point where the two major lines crossed half-way up the cliff on the west side. It wasn't apparent at first, but we realised later it was only a few yards from the stone marker as the crow or seagull flies. We had talked about the strength of the energy vortex at the crossing, and I had the feeling while I was dowsing of my hair standing up at the back of my neck from the influence of an additional energy source.

On subsequent visits I had the opportunity to dowse at this point, cutting out from my mind the effects from the Michael and Mary energies which had seemed to dominate the spot. Almost at once I became aware of two other lines which came in from a north-easterly direction, neatly avoiding the others, crossing and continuing on towards the south-west.

They were equally as strong, but had quite different signatures from the ones we were so used to finding. We have since become convinced that these two pairs of lines are parts of the twelve circles of energy which, according to Druid legend, go round the earth. The sites where these major 'spinal cords' of energy cross are recognisably sacred, and are important points of cosmic energy connection between the earth and the universe. Indeed when meditating on them there is a strong feeling that they have a crucial part to play in the creative process. They can also be the 'portals' through

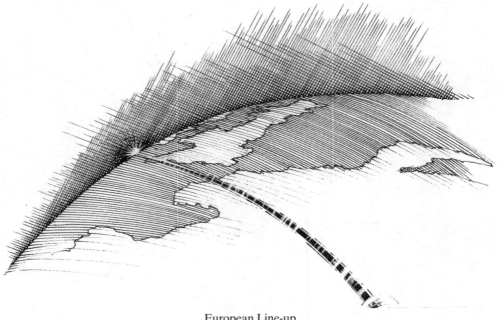

European Line-up

which sensitives from earthside can move to different dimensions, or to allow peripatetic beings of many levels into our frequency to observe us, and perhaps help us develop beyond our current primitive stage.

I believe that what the fishermen saw was a unique event when four lines of multiple frequencies came into resonance to create a powerful vortex of energy which materialised as white light. The explanation makes the happening no less awesome, and it is understandable that many similar manifestations, imbued with religious symbolism and fervour, have given birth to the stuff of legend.

While we were pondering the implications behind the discovery of the two new pulsing energies, John Michell and Christine Rhone's book **Twelve Tribe Nations** fell into our laps. Their interpretation of the work of the Richer brothers Jean and Lucien, who, through inspired dreaming and practical research, established the concept of a St Michael and Apollo Axis stretching from Mt Carmel in the Holy Land to Skellig St Michael in Ireland, sent shivers of anticipation down our spines. Lucien's development of his brother's work on a line centred in Delphi, marking the Virgo-Pisces axis of the Zodiac, led to the discovery of an astonishing alignment of Michael and Apollo sanctuaries across Europe. From Mount Carmel through Lindos, Delos, Athens, Delphi, Kerkyra (Corfu), Monte Gargano, Perugia, Sagra di San Michele, Bourges and Mont St Michel, the line crosses St Michael's Mount before heading off for Skellig St Michael, a little island eight miles off the coast of south-west Ireland. It is a two thousand five hundred mile long sacred pathway between ritual sites.

It had made itself known at St Michael's Mount and we knew we had no alternative but to accept the challenge to follow this newly named Apollo/Athena line wherever it led us.

The Team Prepares

The research on the three hundred mile Mary and Michael line had taken about three years, and the idea of starting out on the prodigious enterprise of dowsing a pair of energy lines for a few thousand miles through Europe was one which needed a little preparatory thought. Paul and I decided to do a few test runs near to the Mount to see if anything exciting might come up.

We might have known.

The weaving Apollo immediately led us a merry dance through important ancient and secret sites, and his counterpart Athena, with quiet authority and dignity, wound her own effortless way through wells, churches and hill forts. The findings in Cornwall alone were worthy of a detailed book and we had only begun to scratch the surface of the project. The team was reinforced by Vivienne Shanley and Ba, whose talents in dowsing, illustration, intuition and research moved the undertaking from a slightly etheric vision to a practical proposition. We committed ourselves to whatever might happen, and from that moment we seemed to be helped in many strange, synchronous ways to get the journey under way.

At first we had to go through all the personality shakedowns to develop the smooth working of the team, and in this we were helped by the natural energies of the earth. We discovered that the four of us were Fire, Air, Earth and Water signs, and the meditations at crossing points became deeply significant in our personal development as we experienced first hand the fundamental effects that powerful earth energies have on our behaviour patterns.

The journey began in November 1992 and is now in the final stages of research. We have been frozen in France ... diving with dolphins ... perspiring in Perugia ... stopped short by snow ... drenched by brown floodwater in Brindisi ... pulled by Policia at the Turin Shroud ... charmed by celestial choirs in cave churches ... saved by squads of Stradali from suspect sinners ... transfixed by traffic in Genoa ... ravaged by rarified mountain air ... dazed by Dodoni ... pooped by the Parthenon ... devastated by Delos ... and constantly exhilarated by the enchantment of finding ancient, forgotten magical legendary places whose elastic energies draw us in to re-establish contact.

The story will be published in a book to follow this one, when we have reached our final goal at Mount Carmel in the Holy Land. Our perceptions are changing as we linger at these powerful sites, and only when we have completed the journey will we begin to understand the message we must convey.

During the first part of the journey we became aware of the many links from Apollo and Athena to other major and minor energy lines around the globe, and the findings have reinforced our original impressions of a simple but sophisticated system of interconnection between all things on earth, and ultimately through the major energy centres to the universe.

In some places it has been clear that the lives of some very advanced people have been influenced by their sensitivity to the energy-flow in their area. The moving story of the relationship between St Francis and his cohort St Clare at Assisi has a remarkable parallel with the behaviour of the energies as they touch many of the sacred places associated with these two highly-evolved gentle people. It took us three days to trace the energy-flows through the exquisitely preserved town from their first dramatic meeting point at the Temple of Minerva until they finally crossed and parted in the ancient crypt under the Duomo. Since we were there Assisi has been hit by serious earthquakes and our thoughts go to those who have suffered in this tragedy.

At San Marco in the Gargano Peninsula we came across the legendary modern miracle worker Padre Pio, who slightly naughtily, because he heartily disliked the long journey to Rome, used to bi-locate when he was summoned by the Pope. With his chuckling charisma he has apparently caused the energies which used to run through his tiny church a hundred yards away to bend round through the new monumental basilica which has been erected in his honour, and where he lies at peace with the universe. It is now a centre for pilgrims and thousands of devoted followers have no doubt influenced the earth's benign flow.

Who says we are not involved in a living, changing, pulsing, dynamic energy system?

WIDENING INTEREST

Back here, in the less exotic but equally interesting unspoiled landscape of the Penwith, we are being contacted more and more by people who are seriously interested in the earth's well-being.

A memorable day was spent with the Netherlands Evangelical Broadcasting Organisation in discussion on earth-energy and dowsing. Apparently the film unit has a fairly broad brief which encourages the investigation of other belief systems for comparison with their own. After preliminary talks the four members of the team took us to Glastonbury and Avebury, where we had a lively good-natured exchange of views from quite widely differing parts of the spectrum. It was a valuable experience for us, as we had to assess every word we said with great care before uttering it, knowing that four very well-informed and articulate people would instantly tear us to pieces if we revealed a weakness of any sort. It certainly clarifies thinking and imposes a severe discipline on the process of explanation. The day went well but inevitably the denouement came at one of the major stones in Avebury, where I was demonstrating the energy patterns round the stones and round the interviewer's quite ample body. I had got to the heart chakra when he quite abruptly asked me who I was working with. I was surprised, at first, because before this all the questions had been searching and constructive.

"With the angelic forces, of course," I said innocently.

There was a mini explosion, the usually verbose interviewer lost for words.

"These energies are evil," he spluttered, "you *cannot* deal with the angelic forces unless you work through Jesus Christ."

I looked at him, the carefully built up rapport collapsing in disbelief.

"You're surely not suggesting that the greater part of the world's population has no access to the angelic realms? *Everybody* has a natural connection to their ultimate creator, and it's just not acceptable any more to say they can't make use of it unless they conform to one particular set of rules."

He didn't want to go any deeper, and for a while we talked subdued pleasantries about their work and what sort of approach they would have to the material we had given them on camera. We left them quaffing a pint in the Red Lion at Avebury, assuring us that we would have a copy of the half-hour programme when they had completed the editing. It duly arrived and perhaps surprisingly proved to be a sensitive and instructive production, including work on ley lines and stones by a Dutch sensitive, until near the end when they managed to find another dowser who was full of doom and gloom about the evil of all earth-energy. Po-faced, and with much head-shaking, he assured the interviewer that whoever was involved in such work was manifestly in liaison with Satan. The last part of the documentary had been in English, and right at the end there was a long-shot of the interviewer by a lovely still pool fed by a gentle stream. He lapsed into Dutch as he stirred the water with a stick. I thought it was rather a neat idyllic ending until I got the translation from a Dutch friend some time later. As the stick went deeper he had said...

"No matter how tranquil and pleasant the surface of the water, when you probe down you always find mud and slime."

I'm afraid he was talking about me.

On hindsight I feel encouraged that the Dutch Evangelists were prepared to consider funding such a programme, and although I heard that most of the reaction to it was of self-righteous outrage that they had not been warned of its inclusion on the agenda, there has been enough response to show that a great number of people are intrigued to learn more about the effects earth-energy has on our lives. Having been involved in a dozen or so similar television programmes over the years I find that the approach to the subject is subtly changing. The time for ridicule and devaluing for the sake of popular viewing has passed, and there are some plans afoot for a rather deeper investigation into the advances made into these and related fields in the last decade. A number of television personalities have dipped a tentative toe into the waters, but they tend to back off as soon as they realise how deep the water might become. I feel that the quest to re-establish our cosmic connections by whatever means is so important that we must make use of the medium of television in any way we can to introduce the potential to a broader spectrum of people. Having done that, we will be able to infuse, through a reawakening of our sense of wonder, a marginally higher commitment to pursuing some of the more rewarding aspects of our lifestyle here.

I had the great privilege and joy of working for a brief period with Kurt Hoffman when he produced and directed *Transformations* for Channel Four a few years ago. It was a brilliant four-part series delicately probing far beyond the usual documentary parameters, and included richly-qualified experts from worldwide fields of science, religion, and philosophy. The approach was inspired. Instead of the usual confrontational technique of trying to provide balance by contrasting opposing viewpoints, Kurt gave the viewer reflective time to consider the implications of each speaker's comments by cutting away to superbly-selected tranquil natural scenes before moving on to the next revelation. He was enabling us to connect to a higher level, but his work was considered by the media gurus either to be ahead of its time, or perhaps of no particular interest to the watching public. I give them the benefit of the doubt, because they did give the series a showing. It came on during mid-afternoons on the four-day run up to Christmas, a time when the viewing audience is probably at its absolute minimum.

Hopefully a more aware Channel Four will have a look through its archives and rediscover this gem. Times have changed and we are hungry for the kind of sensitive programme which can offer inspiration towards a whole new way of thinking.

In many small ways, and through all of our senses, we are re-establishing our delicate links with the universe.

I was pounding hot iron one morning when bouncing into the forge came a smiling man with a copy of **The Sun and the Serpent** in his hand. His enthusiasm was infectious and as we chatted his interest in music and composing stimulated comparisons with our findings of frequencies and vibrations in earth energy. As he left that day to rescue his family from one of the local theme-parks he called over his shoulder that he was going to write a piece of music about the book. I was delighted at his reactions and wondered over the next few weeks whether anything would come of it. I had forgotten all about it when an invitation arrived for us to go to Totnes to hear, amongst a number of other new compositions, the first performance of the piece 'To the Sun and the Serpent'. Here, I must confess, I had visions of a piano and a scraping violin in a draughty village hall, but nevertheless we all poured into a car and arrived to find a large audience already in a packed local church. No scraping violin here, but a sophisticated twenty-eight piece orchestra which seemed well capable of coping professionally with the large number of pieces for which they had only minimal rehearsal time. Ours came in the second half of the concert and we listened still and open-mouthed to ten minutes of descriptive musical delight with a Sibelius-like quality, telling of the coursing energies of the earth, weaving, meeting, and finally parting on their joyous way to greet the universe.

Julian Marshall had truly been inspired by the concepts in the book and we found it a very humbling experience.

He came to the cottage soon after with his family, and expressed a keen interest in dowsing to learn more about earth-energy fields in relation to his work in teaching music. His two children were experimenting with the rods and finding that they actually worked, and it seemed natural that when he asked Ba and me to come to Dartington to chat to his children about dowsing we agreed to do it on their home territory. His 'children' turned out to be the ones in the school, and we found that we were to talk for a whole day to a mixed-bag of about thirty children with an age bracket ranging from six to eleven years old. We arranged separate morning and afternoon sessions and for us it turned out to be a day of rewarding pleasure and a salutary lesson in treating young people as adults. The questions were searching, and needed honest straightforward answers to be accepted. I was explaining the workings of an earth-energy centre which we had dowsed in the classroom with its radials and spiral, and was having difficulty in finding simple words to explain the bits about varying frequencies when a small six year old boy in front, wearing a baseball cap with a huge brim, put his hand up ... they were a refreshingly naturally polite group...

"You mean like the alpha waves in our brains?"

he said, with patient acceptance that I was a bit beyond it.

"Yes, exactly," I said, quickly adjusting my modus operandi to cope with this evidence that they probably knew more than I did.

I had been talking about spending three long years walking and driving, following the Michael and Mary energy lines with a dowsing rod, when a delightful little girl who had been raptly following the story with big wide blue eyes, curly blond hair, and her two front teeth missing, shot up her hand.

"It may be a thilly question," she lisped," but were you able to get home at all during the three years?"

They were an endearing group and we learned a lot. I'm not so sure that we were very popular with the catering people though because at lunchtime the class was already starting to dowse to find which foods were best for them.

RESPONSES TO SOUND

Our work with Julian entered a new phase when he asked if we would help in some work he was doing with a series of musical masterclasses. His idea was that if a class with instrumentalists, composers, singers, dancers, choreographers and other creative people could be exposed to natural earth-energy and its responses, perhaps the creative ability of the individuals or the group would be stimulated, and conversely that the earth-energy might be affected by their input.

We chose the Hurlers, a set of three stone circles at Minions on the edge of Bodmin Moor, for the first trial session and Ba and I explained to the class the nature of the extra dimension they might find in the landscape at this powerful site. Few of them had come across the possibility that the earth might respond to their creative capabilities and it was with some excitement that we approached the ancient stone circle. The earth's energy sensors switched on to the group awareness and we guided the party to a previously-dowsed stone whose energy pattern at rest was marked by a series of pegs. The purpose was to enable them to still their minds, tune in to the stone, and accept whatever it had to give them. They should then respond to the knowledge within the stone, give back whatever they felt they should, then gather at the centre of the circle to express their feelings, each in their own special way.

Gradually they came together and slowly the initial quiet toning developed to chords and resonances which sent primal shivers up and down our spines. As the sounds faded we dowsed the stone to see if there had been any effect. The spiral had wound like a clock-spring to twice its original strength, and a whole new series of radials had developed in response to the communication. Some of the class were able to dowse the effects, and the evidence that they had such a direct connection to the energies of the universe was a profound experience for everyone.

Over a period we have recorded astonishing responses from different groups of people. In one case while tuning and toning round a stone the right-hand spiral gradually unwound, ceased to exist for a moment, then gradually reappeared winding in the opposite direction. On another when the gathering came to the centre there

Cheesewring   P. BROADHURST

was total silence. We thought at first that nothing had happened, then were aware that in silence they were individually expressing deep feelings which could not be translated into sound. One misty day the party left the Hurlers to walk the short distance over to the Cheesewring, a pile of rocks left for some reason at the edge of a great stone quarry and standing proud above the moors, with a presence which suggests that it is not just a natural result of weather erosion.

There were twelve of us that day and all disappeared into the nooks and crannies under the stones leaving no-one visible. I was right underneath at the centre of the rock-pile when I first became aware of the sounds. They grew and welled into breathtaking harmonies as the singing echoed through the minichambers below the stones, and I could feel the very rocks above me vibrating in sonorous movement with these inspired voices. There were tears of joy at the end from the closeness we felt to the earth and to each other. On another day one of the party who had trained with the Gabriella Roth School of Dancing was moved to express her rapport with a powerful group of stones by performing a gravity-defying dance, gliding over the surfaces with the grace of a mountain lion.

Twelve o'clock Rock   H. MILLER

One of the most impressive reactions happened when we developed a series of trials where mind alone is used to communicate with the earth, rather than physical presence. We chose a massive stone known as "the Twelve o'clock rock" on the side of Trencrom to act as our focus and it happily agreed to be involved.

Julian's party were working from their home-base in Devon some hundred miles away, using the same methods as previously but this time concentrating on a photograph of the stone. The stone's energy-field was dowsed at various times in the day, the early morning configuration being taken as the datum for the day. Marginal changes in the field-pattern occur at different times in the twenty-four hours depending on a large number of factors, including moon-cycles and the energy-flow of communicating lines, but normally there are no major shifts in the configuration. Julian never gave a specific time for the meditation but we were always able to pick up on the approximate time by dowsing every two hours to check if anything had happened. The response from the stone at that considerable distance from the group was always positive and significant, and we have recorded a doubling of the energy activity around the centre after the mental linking.

The search for simple ways to strengthen our connections with the earth and the cosmos is on. It is the key to the understanding of creation, and through sound, drumming, colour, meditation, awareness of other energy forms, or whatever, the need to end our isolation from all that is good in the universe is becoming stronger by the day. Our place in the great plan is important and the sooner that more of us get a glimpse of a more balanced way to live as individuals and groups, the sooner our domestic, social and political problems will be reduced to their proper level.

Chapter Fifteen

QUO VADIS

PERHAPS ONE OF the great dilemmas we have to contend with is the firmly entrenched belief that nothing can really be done about social, religious, political, national, ethnic and monetary problems because they have become so huge.

It is quite simply *not true*.

Most of us have a pretty good idea of how we would like the world to be. We are constantly taken aback and saddened when, according to our television or newspapers, other people don't seem to share the same view. Our sensibilities are battered into submission by endless reports of violence in every field and we become anaesthetised and incapable of appreciating the wonderful things going on all round us. There is a feeling of vulnerability and foreboding and for the moment the 'doom and gloom' brigade seem to have got the upper hand.

There is absolutely no need for this mind set to continue.

The most powerful people on earth have no more capacity to dominate than you or I unless very large numbers of us agree to go along with them. Amongst them are charismatic organisers who skilfully bind groups together, offering security in the shape of status, political stability, religion, or the provision of finance in return for a perpetuation of their image. In its initial stages this practice is perfectly acceptable and a comfort to most of us. 'Belonging' becomes an important part of our social structure and leads to growing confidence and strength in the individual. Problems start, however, when these leaders lose sight of their purpose here on earth and start to widen their base to influence or take over neighbouring groups. Power is a heady business and its pursuit demands decisions which recognise less and less the value of caring for people or the earth we live on.

Pressure from business, political, financial and religious bodies has increased beyond the safety limit and we are now contending with the worst scenario in terms of manipulation of our lifestyles in our history. Perhaps with the new values engendered by a fuller understanding of our symbiotic relationship with the earth, we can take an eagle's-eye view of what is happening to this wonderful planet and all the beings living on it. An eagle can spot a rabbit five kilometres away, so in human terms we need a fundamental change in our perception for us to evolve further than our present myopic vision allows. This is not an incitement for yet another peasant revolt to overthrow unpopular landlords, replacing the old system with another one which is quite liable to be equally bad, but a positive way of guiding our future, *using existing structures*, by subtly influencing the thought processes of the people at the top. We can all be involved, each person's contribution being as valuable as any other, and it can be done with dignity and honesty. We don't need crude, artificial aids like newspapers, television screens, or sophisticated electronically-controlled communications systems to convey our simple message. Happily most of us now reject the idea that the only way to get through to people is to shout very loudly and, if they don't listen, beat them soundly round the ears.

Each one of us has access to a universal, powerful force for good which will harm no one. It comes from direct contact with the Management who work at very different frequencies and time scales from us, and cannot interfere in our affairs until we ask. They look for the simplest change which will lead to the required result, and sometimes we can only understand the strange way they operate by looking back in time to appreciate the sweet logic of the subtle changes they have made. We are all

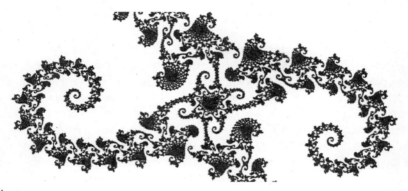

Fractals   DAVID MUMFORD

part of the creative life force, and with their help and guidance, we can take positive steps towards a more rewarding and fulfilling life-style. Thousands of people round the world are taking part in meditations, meetings, ceremonies, therapies and discussions to increase their awareness and make them more conscious of spiritual values. For me, dowsing was the path that led me to deeper understanding of human need, but any of the other disciplines are equally valid if they make us aware of our real potential. Our thought processes along with those from the earth and the universe carry into global consciousness, the combined input far beyond the restrictions of our human problems. Embodied in this vibrant storehouse is a vast font of knowledge and experience available to us all when we start our journey out of the chaos we have engendered in our physical world. Advanced mathematicians, whom I once considered dry old sticks, have been working with inspired theories of probabilities and perception which led us to the understanding that there is logic in chaos. They've moved on now through the apparent disorder to discover the endlessly harmonic beauty of fractals, and their work makes me feel strongly that our present cycle is a precursor of idyllic times to come.

How Do We Start?

Perhaps before we learn to use the power of thought, we ought to clarify our thinking on exactly what our problems are, and from deep inside ourselves question the validity of arguments in favour of sustaining the status quo. Are the people who make major decisions which seriously affect our lifestyles really qualified to make them? Are judgments made with care and consideration and not *too* influenced by the figures on the bottom line of the accounts? Who *are* the people who decide what is good for us and the planet? Will they come forward and be accountable for the results of their actions? We have the right, and indeed the obligation, to make our own judgments on all of these matters provided we are coming from the right place. And the right place is quite simply love and concern for our earth home and the people around us.

PINNING THE PROBLEMS

Our habitat is being threatened by a number of well-established systems under the headings of ... 'business and financial practice' ... 'religious dogma' ... and 'political expediency'. It is now almost impossible to consider them as operating separately, and they must now accept a collective responsibility to reconsider their priorities.

International conglomerates control enough money to install whoever they need in positions of political strength. It has gone a long way beyond a few backhanders to existing political figures, to a level, particularly in America, which pretty well guarantees that few people can afford to put themselves up for nomination without substantial sponsorship from one or another of the large corporations. It's hardly surprising that fewer than forty-five percent of the USA's population actually voted in the last election. Most of them know perfectly well what is going on and made it abundantly clear that all was not well in the forum. Authors like Gore Vidal have launched well-researched, blistering attacks on the immorality of many of the commercial decisions made by multinational companies. Some of these have disturbing political and environmental consequences, and debate is being opened by concerned people throughout the world to consider alternative ways to safeguard our quality of life.

Amongst these global businesses, the ultimate behemoth, violent, fearsome, predatory and without a thought for anything but itself, the dreaded Tyrannosaurus Rex of all the dinosaurs, is undoubtedly the oil business, with its equally ferocious and dependent partner, the motor car industry. The power of their lobby in America was transparently obvious during the recent world-wide efforts to reduce carbon dioxide emissions from vehicles.

Our profligate use of oil has been responsible for a greater part of the destruction of the environment and the creation of more stressful living conditions than any other single factor in our history. The burning of fossil fuels destroys our delicately balanced atmosphere. Chemical by-products from its processing, now used excessively in agriculture, are obliterating the natural functions of our top-soil, and eventually leach into our water supplies, rivers and oceans. In the name of efficiency, by the use of artificial fertilisers, crops are induced to grow so fast that our wheat hasn't got time to absorb the vital trace elements from the earth which are essential for our well-being. Wars have been fought, vast tracts of land have been rendered sterile, and some very suspect financial and political deals have been made to ensure the continued consumption of this profitable commodity.

Motor car designers, manufacturers and marketeers have combined in a frenetic effort to make people buy new concepts of cars. They have recently managed to implant the notion that if children cannot be driven to school in a gas-guzzling, four-wheel-drive, macho, semi-truck with fitted bull-bars, mummy will feel socially deprived. This is surely a reflection of both the irresponsibility of an entire industry which is perfectly well aware of the mounting problems of transportation, and of our human weakness which allows marketing forces to dictate how we behave. Traffic problems in all major cities in the world have already reached gridlock proportions, and pollution, stress and needlessly wasted time are the fall-out from our obsession with the motor car.

While we protest loudly and long about being exposed to an odd new disease which can at worst affect a minimal number of people, we are quite remarkably silent when confronted by figures on the appalling carnage we have come to accept on our roads. A look at statistics from The Royal Society for the Prevention of Accidents for 1995—there are no collated results later than this at the time of going to press—is enough to send shivers of horror down the spine.

In the United Kingdom alone, three thousand six hundred and twenty-one people were killed on the roads.

This is just under *ten people a day*.

In addition, forty five thousand, five hundred and twenty-three were *seriously* injured.

This is nearly *one hundred and twenty-five a day*.

An additional *two hundred and fifty-seven thousand, seven hundred and forty-one* were injured to a lesser degree but will probably be traumatised for life.

This is another *seven hundred and six every day*.

The figures for America show that *one hundred and eleven people* were killed *every* day on their roads during 1994.

These are just bald statistics of accidents and take no account of the grief, distress and shock to all the families and friends of the victims.

All of us are perhaps guilty of ignoring these tragedies because we feel that the freedom to have personal transport is now an essential part of living, and it would be too much of a retrograde step to suggest withdrawing that freedom. However, while it's right to enable people to have a form of individual transport, no one has the right to choose a method of transport which has developed, through our aggression, selfishness and downright stupidity, into a killing machine.

WHAT ON EARTH CAN WE DO?

The eagle soaring above us, seeing the overall picture much more clearly, but unaware of the strange, misguided social pressures to own a bigger and faster car to symbolise our life-success rating, would point a talon immediately to high-speed travel as a major contributory factor to our problems.

To *initiate* a solution, a simple logical step might be taken. Let's put it out to the planetary consciousness that a global law be passed to limit the top speed for any vehicle to 56mph. Shrieks and wails would no doubt issue from everyone who had not yet been involved in an accident about the importance of personal freedom. I defend the right to individual choice vehemently, but in my book the right to kill and injure does not come into the equation. A number of benefits would immediately be apparent. At this speed petrol engines are near their most efficient performance in terms of fuel consumption, so we start with a considerable reduction in atmospheric pollution. Lower speeds would reduce the numbers of accidents, and the results of these would be less severe. Stress factors would be lowered by adopting a more leisurely rate of travel. Of course we would need to be educated to re-arrange our lives to compensate for slightly longer journeys. Those who have to travel to work from long distances would have to get up five minutes earlier and perhaps arrive more refreshed in the gentler traffic to deal with the day's problems. Until people got used to the idea, stringent speed checking could be introduced to make sure that *no-one* except the emergency services was allowed to travel at high speeds. Drivers who exceeded the limits would stick out like a sore thumb and it would not take long for us to develop an acceptance of reduced speed as part of a more rewarding and relaxing life-style.

The shift of emphasis away from speed capability would trigger new design concepts of a vehicle for personal transport. Safety, comfort, and low and alternative fuel consumption would be substituted for the '0-60 mph in five seconds' mentality which has reigned for too long. Perhaps even the oil companies could be persuaded to part with some of the millions they have made to research and develop new and friendlier means of staying mobile. I'm sure that private entrepreneurs would see investment opportunities in providing special tracks with skid pans and hairy corners where people who get a buzz from fast driving can play all day to their hearts' content. Well-run railways could take back a great deal of bulk transport, with short-range electric or alternatively-powered vehicles delivering from terminals. Friendlier neighbours might encourage more car-sharing, and more efficient and better funded Park-and-Drive systems help to create pleasant pedestrian walkways and shopping areas. The need for really efficient public transport would become an interesting new avenue for research, and application of cash resources with an emphasis on relaxed journeys would help to change our perceptions of what we *really* need in terms of personal carriers.

We can help to move events like these to fruition by projecting our positive thoughts to the universal consciousness. During my stint as a designer I became acutely aware of the way this works. I remember spending three years designing the 'perfect' chair. Came the day when I was satisfied with the endless prototypes and ready to put it into production. I sat down to relax, quietly browsing through an American furniture magazine. To my absolute consternation and anguish, I saw in one of the exhibition features a superb colour picture of an almost identical chair about to be marketed in the USA. I have since come across many inventions, books, designs and medical breakthroughs which appear simultaneously thousands of miles apart with no discernable connection, and am convinced that ideas going into the ether become available to others at the same level of creative thought. There is no reason why this effective means cannot be used in sensitively orchestrated stages to provide people who make major decisions with a wider and more compassionate understanding of the deeper issues involved in their judgements. 'Global consciousness' is where minds meet when they are released from the constricting bonds of social, cultural and ethnic programming. Free from prejudice they can consider alternative ideas, accept the reasoning behind them, and come to balanced conclusions in the light of a new breadth of knowledge. Even the hardest power-seekers have moments when their minds, perhaps in half-waking sleep, move into this area, and they will be irrevocably influenced by finding the thought patterns we have projected. These are immensely powerful and permanent and are immeasurably stronger than the fleeting, transitory forms created from negative

The Hopi Storyteller   PRISSIE HOLWILL

thinking. It may take time, but previously rigid minds will inexorably change to encompass a degree of compassion. Eventually, as perceptions expand, values will change as they find infinitely better rewards in developing true friendships, love, caring for less talented members of our society, and renewing their rapport with the earth and everything on it. The more energy we put into these thoughts the more likely they are to become possibilities. Increased energy makes any possibility a probability, and with just a little extra push it becomes an event. I've never subscribed to the notion so often expressed that 'if it's meant, it will happen'.

'It' only comes to fruition with the sustained application of energy.

ANOTHER DINOSAUR

We are temporarily trapped by marketing forces into a system of food supply in the Western world which, in the name of efficiency, seems hell-bent on the destruction of any concept of life in a close-knit community. At first the prospect of being able to do most of one's shopping under one roof seemed like a good idea, but the downside of the social disruption created by the system is becoming a serious problem. We are losing our sense of identity in communities which have no living centres, no points of contact, no relaxed meeting places, no pride in being part of a progessive living group. Until out-of-town shopping in supermarkets developed, people still had a chance to chat to each other and exchange news in the local village shops – large towns and cities are collections of villages – but the growth of national consortiums of retailers, building societies and banks has led to a boring sameness throughout the country in our shopping areas which has destroyed our unique, precious local quality of life. A very important person in the settlements and villages of the indigenous Americans was their story-teller, whose life's work was to gather children together and tell them the stories and legends of their ancestors, their land, their myths and their gods. It gave them a sense of belonging, of pride, of being an important part of the tribe and understanding its ways. It gave them a feeling of dignity, acceptance of life and an awareness of each one's personal relationship with the earth and the cosmos. It was important for both the individual and the group.

For years large companies have been engaged in getting rid of competition from small private shops by undercutting prices, and the resultant bulk-buying by supermarket cartels has put thousands of juggernauts on the roads carting food products half-way round the world before they reach our tables. Now that the competition has all but gone, refined calculations on profitability are defining what we are allowed to eat. Many a time a polite enquiry for a favourite item is met with a terse ... 'There's no call for that now, sir,' ... which really means, apart from implying that I am a bit old-fashioned, that the turnover for that product per square metre of shelf space is not high enough to justify stocking it.

One thing we do well in Cornwall is grow cauliflowers—'broccoli' to the locals. Last year our farmers had to plough a large part of the crop back into the ground. The regional supermarkets imported them from Spain 'because they were smaller and whiter' and could not, or would not, make any purchases from neighbourhood farmers. Multiply this statistical stupidity a million times around the world and you create a nightmare of wasted time, energy, money, and a veritable fog of pollution so that this particular dinosaur needn't divert from its lumbering course. Encouragingly there was such a furore about the broccoli, leading to a considerable reduction in supermarket sales, that one of the larger groups has made contracts with Cornish farmers for the supply of vegetables this year. We are beginning to learn the power of simply saying... No! A little consideration at top levels and a clause in regional planning permission would ensure that farmers and growers had automatic access to at least a part of every supermarket store for the sale of locally grown supplies.

The eagle, in his wisdom, would look at the existing set-up and our burgeoning technology and almost certainly suggest that supermarkets could develop in the future as simple warehouses where we could buy the mundane and weighty part of our shopping like potatoes, flour, sugar, spare tins, toilet rolls, soap powder, nappies, whisky, and all the boring routine necessities of life through a computer. If I didn't own one I would be happy to do the job in a terminal set up for the purpose in a comfortable cafe, and have my shopping delivered by electric vehicle to my door. There would be huge savings in time, costs of packaging and incalculable improvements in pollution and stress from cars. Communities could again have specialist shops in a refurbished Village Street where the butcher, cheesemonger, baker, veg and fruiterer, clothier, ironmonger, deli and grocer, watchmaker, shoe and sports vendor, fishmonger, liquor store and newsagent would have a real knowledge of their business and a genuine interest in what their customers really want. Shopping could be revitalised as a pleasant social occasion, a light-hearted family event, looking for special things which merit some discussion, establishing easy human contact and building a sense of community. It applies equally to inner cities as much as country towns, would engender a sense of civic pride in the local environment, and perhaps provide some relief from the agonising loneliness of so many people in our present isolated society.

There are many problems which can be tackled in a similar way, using existing structures and finding solutions by initiating simple changes in thought patterns. We all have a part to play in recognising the weaknesses of our society and taking positive action to achieve improvements. An enormous energy reserve is ready in the universe to help in moving our materially-oriented society to a more rewarding phase. The Management are there to offer gentle guidance to those who are sensitive to the earth's needs. The process has already started, and as more minds tune in to the creation of a peaceful and relaxed way of living the momentum will grow irresistibly. If these concepts are introduced subtly into the minds of controlling authorities or businessmen, and they actually initiate changes leading to a happier and more spiritually aware society, they can rejoice in the belief that they did it themselves ... and why not? As long as it works, it's fine!

There are signs that the business world is beginning to listen to the whispered messages from the ether. The Director-General of the Institute of Directors in a recent address to the members said it is 'Time for a New Morality in Business'. His concern was that companies should conduct their affairs so that the non-business community could trust them again. The old ways of Weinstock, who finally lost control of GEC through his obsession with short- term returns for shareholders rather than expansion and job creation through research and development, are on the way out. The days when everything is costed and nothing valued are numbered as more aware people take back their powers of decision. The latest courses on business development are majoring on replacing cost-accounting with value-accounting where 'value' includes intellectual, social and community benefits from the product. Manufacturers and service industries are becoming conscious that they need support from the rest of the community, and it's encouraging to find that a number of them have primed the pumps for regeneration projects, particularly in the inner cities, towns and villages which have been hit hardest by changing manufacturing techniques.

There are still, of course, many very large conglomerates who operate globally outside ethical boundaries. The Murdochs of this world still arrange to have their 'Registered Offices' in whichever country of the world is prepared to present them with the lowest tax bill. Their empires return practically nothing to the communities who support them, and their cynical accounting systems mean that governments lose revenue in countless millions which could well be used to improve our social services. Dedicated barristers, of course, earn personal fortunes proving that the complex financial machinations are within the confines of International Law.

Most of us have a deep-down sense of fair play. We moan, but eventually we pay our taxes and contribute to the cost of living in a society where the less fortunate need help in coping with their lives. In the old days people used to pitch in by fishing, hunting, collecting firewood or carrying water for those who couldn't, so there's nothing new in the idea. At that time in the smaller communities there was no place for the crook who might hi-jack the fish from the chaps who caught it, and corner the market. He would have had pretty short shrift from the fishermen. Let's become more aware of some of these international fiddles which apparently are still acceptable by the establishment. We can put it out to the universe that we would like to see a level playing-field in the realms of taxation, and if it needs a few honest politicians around the world with the tenacity of a top American criminal lawyer of the calibre of Scheck (but without his immorality!) to get their teeth firmly into these financial charlatans, then so be it.

DREAMTIME?

A dreamer? Another impractical idealist? Nonsense! I'm a seventy-year-old horny-handed practical blacksmith who has had the great joy of feeling what it's like to be in the presence of beings who think and act in a very different way from us humans. We don't have to die to communicate with them. The knowledge is within us now, and is slowly being released through higher levels of perception. Look for the winds of change. In spite of the depressing news on television and in newspaper headlines we are in the midst of exciting transformations which will shape the contours of a happier society. Have a look at *Positive News*, a paper providing an invigorating, stimulating breath of fresh air in a smog-ridden newspaper world. It's a joy to discover in its pages the hundreds of thousands of people from every walk of life who *do* care. Their work is inspirational, their efforts mostly unsung until more of us find a deeper meaning in our lives. Their vision is for a dynamic, active, forward-looking society with the spiritual capacity to relate naturally to each other, and nurture the wonderful planet which gives us all life and provides us with our every need. We are all searching for a more profound understanding of our inner feelings. The depth of our capacity for compassion was briefly apparent at the time of Princess Diana's death. Open outpourings of genuine personal grief, quite unparalleled in history, across the whole spectrum of society throughout the world revealed deep yearnings to understand more fully our place in the universe. The overwhelming response was triggered by her simple capacity for genuine caring and love, and the event had a crucially important effect on our collective psyche. We all have untouched potentials within us which sometimes are released only as a result of a traumatic shock.

GOOD REASONS FOR OPTIMISM

Who would have thought that the removal of the Berlin Wall could have happened with such astonishing speed and with only a fraction of the anticipated stress? Did anyone really believe that the South African apartheid question could be resolved without horrendous bloodshed?

Of *course* there are still residual problems to be sorted out in both these cases, but in principle, people are engaged in *talking* about solutions rather than beating each other's heads in. Hopefully the endless patience of the negotiators in Ireland will result in an acceptable society for all parties to live together happily. Except for a few unbalanced extremists everyone has a desperate need for stability in the Province. Stability means freedom from fear and the safe, peaceful enjoyment of your chosen way of life. It doesn't seem a lot to ask. Perhaps we could infiltrate the thought into the minds of fanatical supporters of both sides that there's some merit in accepting that the other fellow might have a legitimate point of view?

The religious rifts in the Middle East, again exacerbated by small minorities, are potentially explosive. With boundless restraint negotiators try to talk their way through the minefields of difficulties, bending over backwards to avoid using gunboat diplomacy to find solutions. It's a huge step forward, and as these delicate discussions go on there is no doubt that the intrusion of religious and national hype from newspapers does not help. Extremists of all colours and creeds have one fundamental weakness in common — a lack of compassion. We can help soften their rigid mind-sets by introducing to the global consciousness a fresh expanding energy of thoughtfulness, of consideration, of the courtesy and respect which was a measure of how the old people felt for the earth and everything on it.

Perhaps in the extreme case of Saddam Hussein, we could adopt a ploy used by the defence in a recent National Lottery Court action. The accused had been found guilty of some serious misdemeanours and was about to be sacked. His lawyer, apparently undismayed, said that his client "had decided to advance his planned retirement"! It's an interesting way out and I'm sure the Management with their wry sense of humour would actively support its introduction to the planetary consciousness with particular reference to Saddam.

A QUESTION OF RELIGION

Most of us know little of the sacred beliefs of the many religions available to us except the one we were introduced to as a child. It is a refreshing experience to spend time at the St Mungo Museum of Religion in Glasgow with its splendid presentations of each religion's basic history and doctrines. To begin with, because of the numerous sects, schisms, and emphases, it seems that they are irreconcilable, but as you absorb the details and are able to cross-refer easily in the gallery, it becomes clear that the differences at grassroots level between Christianity, Islam, Judaism, Hindu, Sikhism, Buddhism and all the other major religions are minimal. We all walk along different paths, but with the growth of mixed ethnic communities there is now a much greater opportunity to meet,

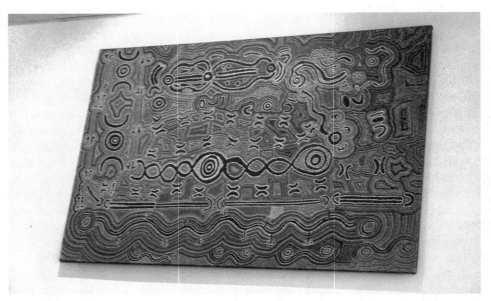

Kangaroo Wild Cabbage   ST MUNGO MUSEUM, GLASGOW

discuss, and possibly begin to understand the nuances which may be important to one or other party.

Christians preach love of fellow humans ... Islam promotes brotherhood ... Taoism is about harmony with nature ... and Buddhists are quiet, contemplative and aware of mystical energies ... Aboriginals know that the land is alive with the meaning and power of their ancestors who, in the Dreamtime, established the laws on how to live.

The simple messages have been all but destroyed over the years as men lost sight of the innocent truths behind them. We have built such immense structures to celebrate them that the sound, solid foundations have disappeared from view. In Britain we are having an agonising reappraisal of our religious behaviour and beliefs which is stirring up powerful feelings on the need for change. The movement is not anti any particular religion, but expresses a yearning for spiritual enlightenment from a source which accepts social change and does not depend on fear and dogma for its discipline. Our perceptions have altered over the last two thousand years, and it would seem that rapidly reducing congregations are an indication that our needs are no longer being met by the establishment. Church leaders of all denominations recognise this and are taking steps to respond, but it is understandable that after hundreds of years of established doctrinal discipline, any movement in relaxing the rigid controls on both shepherd and flock must be gradual. Many people within the Church hierarchy and in the congregations feel threatened by any proposed alterations in the familiar procedures, but there are positive signs now that the restricting, controlling bonds which have gagged forward-thinking clergy for so long are beginning to loosen.

It's obvious that many priests who gave lip service to the stringent rules of conduct were independent enough to make their own decisions about some things. In *Montaillou*, an intimately descriptive book by Emmanuel Le Roy Ladurie on Cathars and Catholics in a French village in the late thirteenth and early fourteenth centuries, the local priest Pierre Clergue decided that the rules of priestly celibacy ceased to apply at an altitude of 1300 metres! Above that height he became a 'womaniser par excellence', and as he lived in the Pyrenees he seemed to have considerable opportunity. Nearer our own times in the fifties and sixties, Padre Pio, whose shrine is now visited by five million pilgrims a year, is reputed to have 'summoned women disciples to his hut by signalling with a red lantern'. According to 'L'Espresso' magazine, a Vatican official who had been asked to investigate the rumours sent a message to the Pope of the day that "bis in hebdomade copulabat cum muliere" ... a loose translation of which is that he copulated with women twice a week! His shadow has grown no less because of his reputed misdemeanours, and these human 'failings' have probably made him more acceptable to those followers who attend to confess their sins.

It seems to me that truly spiritual growth by individuals in direct contact with their creator is a desirable way ahead for humanity in the future. Religions which are prepared to accept change, and respond to our evolving needs will continue to play an important part in shepherding us through times of difficulty as we move out from the cosy protection of our familiar religious umbrellas. We may feel vulnerable for a while, but as we tune in to the energies of the earth and everything on it, seen and unseen, and feel its connections to the universe, we will begin to recognise all of our gods as manifestations of different aspects of the life-force. We humans are part of this unity, and it is patently absurd for us to continue to squabble over the technical details of how we connect with it.

A clear message now to the planetary consciousness that we are all heading in the same direction, on different pathways, might help to avoid some local stumbling as we progress on our way.

THE OTHER SIDE OF DYING

We've never really been able to talk openly enough about dying. It's odd really because it's the one certainty we have in our otherwise unstable lives. The contemplation of it is hedged with fear and superstition though you would think that its inevitablility would allow us to prepare ourselves for it at an early stage so that we can accept it with equanimity when it comes, and get on with enjoying our slice of life here while we can. Many Buddhists move close to this way of living. The fourteenth century Tibetan Buddhist Longchenpa wrote...

Since everything is but an apparition
Perfect in being what it is
Having nothing to do with good or bad
Acceptance or rejection
One may well burst out in laughter.

What a joyous, health-giving way of dealing with our strange lives here.

There are lots of ways of preparing for death, but I do not believe for a moment that our life should be entirely spent in an elaborate ritualistic preparation for the next one. We will not qualify by flagellating ourselves, or piously chanting 'Mea Culpa', or endlessly confessing that we are terrible sinners. Whichever divinity we are praying to would quite justifiably be bored stiff after the first few sessions. The real preparation for moving on is in the way we respond every moment to interactions with everything that touches our lives.

When someone you love dies they leave a gap which can never be filled. The pain of bereavement is deep and searching and difficult to bear. The greater the love the more difficult it is to come to terms with living on without them, and while time helps to heal the rawest wounds it can't, and shouldn't, erase the memory. They have moved to a place where you can no longer experience their physical presence, but they are still as real as they ever were. Their essence, enriched by their new experience, goes on and will be recognisable although not in physical form when your time comes to join them.

But you still have your own unique life to lead, lessons to learn, experiences to be enjoyed, connections to make, work to do on your spiritual and mental development and, in time, the satisfying enjoyment of the rich tapestry of life. The whole burden of grief is always with those left behind, and perhaps some alleviation of the sorrow can come from an absolute knowledge that whoever dies has the choice to stay on in a wonderful place, or come back to learn a bit more before moving on.

It's hard to get rid of a lurking fear of dying and perhaps being prodded into the flames by a chap with a trident and a forked tail. This idea only exists in the minds of people who still subscribe to the belief that we have to suffer to become pure. It's pretty plain by now that the whole concept was introduced by some of the old religious manipulators who used this threat to keep us peasants from getting stroppy. 'Death' is a transition by the life-force from one phase to another. The essence, or soul, or whatever name you are comfortable with, in most cases leaves its temporary host for a period of quiet contemplation before moving on to its next cycle. During this time it is nurtured and cared for by angelic forces who freely encompass all of our religions without prejudice. Their love and concern is palpable and my experience with them and their gentle strength stays with me through every day of my life, firing me with the need to pass on this magical knowledge in any way I can, however inept. We have lost the old ways of ritual preparation for dying, when people understood the moving-on of spirit and essence, and the overcoming of our fear is the first step we can make towards a peaceful transformation.

There is real joy in the knowledge that death is the start of a fascinating and challenging new life.

THERE'S ALWAYS A TEASPOON

My sister Ivy was staying with us for a short holiday recently and had volunteered to do the washing-up after our evening meal. We were all chatting quietly and as she poured the water from the washing-up bowl there was a little 'clunk' from the sink. "There's always a teaspoon!" she said with resignation, and with a wry smile fished it out and dealt with it. It struck me as a cameo of most of our lives. No matter how well we organise ourselves and anticipate the problems of the day, some unexpected things are liable to happen to upset the even tenor of our way. Sometimes they are quite trivial, often disconcerting, occasionally traumatic, but they are all there as part of a learning process that fine-hones us to clearer perceptions. The more we can deal with them with humour and understanding, the easier they are to handle. We all begin like simple pieces of iron, which under a master's hand, can be heated and caressed into something beautiful by the successive, sometimes forceful, sometimes gentle hammer-blows of experience.

It's difficult to emulate the eagle when most of us are living on month to month resuscitation with a wary eye on financial survival, but even a quick venture out to probe into the things we find really fulfilling is immeasurably rewarding. Prozac-weary financial and business people are turning to organisations like the National Retreat Association to find sanctuaries where the emphasis is on personal quiet and inner reflection rather than yet another quick-fix course. There is a movement towards the value of growing spiritually as well as financially. Some of them could learn quite a lot from the Local Exchange Trading System (LETS), an honest, low-level, practical method of energy exchange geared to rebuilding communities and providing opportunities for meeting new people . It's a system that encourages individual effort and encompasses the heartfelt need for social contact beyond the Cellnet and bar-stool. It's non-political and non-profit-making, and that's not a bad recommendation in itself.

In every field of human endeavour minds with rigidly held views are mellowing, becoming more aware, and opening to accept values which had previously been obscured by prejudice. In the realms of architecture, advanced thinkers of the calibre of Keith Critchlow understand the importance of sacred geometry, and are interpreting its mystical significance in the creation of exciting new buildings. New technology in astronomy and physics is revealing the unimaginable immensity of the universe, while discovering that the elements we humans are made of are fairly commonly distributed around the galaxies. Given a cocktail of a few odd bits of metal, carbon, hydrogen and oxygen, the last two separately and in the form of living water, heated, shaken but not stirred, it seems that there are billions of places where another life-form like us could be holding forth on how unique they are. Scientists are continually crossing boundaries of knowledge, giving wider scope to our spiritual development. It's an exciting time to live, as new discoveries confirm that we are truly part of the great creative force of the universe. As individuals we can take on the responsibility for our own patch, and as the human race we can surely consider the earth as our own backyard. We have played an uncaring part in destroying its delicate infrastructure particularly over the last hundred years, and in the coming millenium we can't sit back and wait for it to regenerate while we continue to behave so badly. It needs our help to get back to its natural rhythmic harmony. We are learning that planetary consciousness is the common ground in our symbiotic relationship, and we must respond to the earth's anguish with love, the true religion of the people.

The male of the species is becoming more sensitive and the females are recovering their strength. We are striving for the delicate balance between them which has eluded us for generations. We are taking back our power to make our own decisions, and with it the strength to take on the responsibility for them. In the Monterey Bay Aquarium there is a gigantic two-storey window and from different levels you can watch lazily swimming sharks, exotic fish, languid crabs and all the denizens of a living kelp forest in their natural surroundings. There is a dramatic entrance where you walk into a sort of upside-down glass pudding-bowl. Inside it's blacked-out except for a three-foot wide strip of clear curved glass near the top. Thousands of brilliantly lit anchovies swim endlessly clockwise round the bowl, a mesmeric sight against the light green background.

We could feel the energy from their eternal circular chase for food and were about to leave when we were stopped short by the sight of one single maverick fish, stationary apart from a few deft wriggles of a tail fin, and pointing in the opposite direction from all the rest. She had made her decision, ignoring the rushing, urgent, headlong, unthinking conformity of all her peers, and sat there, effortlessly eating as food was brought to her by the swift current. We hugged ourselves in appreciation

The Maverick

of what she was doing and laughed outright in acknowledgement of her fierce independence. Laughter and enthusiasm are seriously infectious, and it was not long before an entire group of observers were grinning and gesticulating in delighted recognition of her statement. Medical experts have discovered that the act of laughing activates all sorts of healthy input to our chemical and electrical systems, so the feel-good factor after a good belly laugh has a great influence on the way we look at the world.

The other day I was driving along the A30 a few miles from Penzance when I saw a group of seven or eight girls walking along the footpath. As I got near they all turned round and smiled and waved. I smiled and waved back and in the rear mirror

I saw them do the same with a following car. They had no motive other than the joy of life and I could see the responsive grin on the face of the driver. I suddenly felt happy and everyone seemed to be much more pleasant as I did my few bits of business in the town. On the way back I was aware of a smiling line of drivers coming towards me, and passed the same group of girls still waving and laughing as they walked along. They gave so much pleasure to many people on their journey that day with a simple wave and smile ... it didn't cost anything and had a more exhilarating effect than any drug.

There are simple lessons to learn in so many ways. Be a maverick sometimes and make your decisions not in the light of previous experience but in recognition of a new aware intuition. It will not be selfish because a true intuitive process involves care and concern for your environment and the people around you. Smile and say 'Hello' to someone... rediscover the joy of the dancing nuances of the human voice. Do a Wordsworth ... develop a 'religious' rapport with the landscape, and realise you are at one with it. Recognise your own potential.

My little Sequoia Sempervirens is now twenty-seven inches high, and she's beginning to believe what I tell her. Like most of us she has gone through some rough experiences ... I put her outside in the summer thinking that she would find the Cornish sun refreshing with her Californian origin, but after a couple of days I found her bedraggled, brown and wilting. I was destraught but some tender loving care at last reassured her, restored her green foliage, and she's that much tougher for the experience. She also had her top shoot knocked off by our massive Bernese Mountain dog's tail, but a side branch has taken over now and there's hardly a kink to show for it. We've reached an agreement that she won't be put outside till she's four feet high and good and ready. Beyond that she holds her vision of standing tall, held in the earth, accepting her sustenance and in return nurturing a great symbiotic vortex of energy with the earth as part of their connection with the universe.

Sequoia's Grandma

The Final Step   H. MILLER

We can all have dreams, triggered in our subconscious by release from our five-sense bindings, and the ability to have such visions is already pre-programmed within us.

We are hovering on the brink of great changes. As the millenium approaches many are aware that a paradigm shift in our perceptions is imminent. This is not a dress rehearsal. We are about to experience the combined effects of myriads of subtle changes over a long period. It is a time of joy and anticipation, not for fear. The transition will be simple. The glue that holds us all together is love.

We have built solid foundations through meditation, prayer, a belief in the continuity of life and an understanding of our purpose here on earth.

We are stretching our minds to touch new concepts, and the Management are reaching out to us, responding to our needs. We have the courage and vision to close the gap. We can do it quietly, a little at a time. Possibly the changes we will trigger may not come in our own time here; but what better gift can we make to future generations than to contribute to the preservation of our home planet?

It's time to move forward, to take the final step ... now.

The earth is waiting.

It's not too late.

EPILOGUE

The little energy centre in my sitting room has not been idle in the last few months. She is trying to get down to my level to start a dialogue of simple communication. I feel inadequate to interpret the subtleties of what she is trying to convey, but know no other way to converse with her other than by dowsing her responsive, vibrant, moving biomagnetic fields. I feel some of her manifestations stirring dusty chambers in my mind, and at these times there is an elusive familiarity and almost a recognition of her language. Then, probably because my rational mind interferes, I lose the sense of her message and am aware of her patient acceptance that we must try again. There is a haunting intimacy in our rapport, and sometimes the veil between us is so thin that the frustration of not being able to make full contact is difficult to bear.

Not long ago I was working with Ted Seaton, a sensitive Geordie with an acute awareness of earth energies and a nose for delving into the ancient history of the countryside. While we were chatting I became fascinated by the amulet he was wearing on a leather cord round his neck. He had found the tiny stone in the early eighties while researching a bronze age settlement on Scargill High Moor amongst thousands of tons of rocks, and had picked it up because he noticed a hole in it. It was covered with green lichen, and it was only when he got it home and cleaned it that he found an exquisitely incised face on the end opposite the hole. American and

British experts have studied the artefact and have ascribed various dates up to 900BC, most of them acknowledging that it is probably a representation of a Celtic God. The face is no more than 25mm long and 13mm wide and is inscribed in meticulous detail in very hard stone.

The Seaton Amulet   T. SEATON

Even before I'd heard the story of its authenticity I could feel stimulating energy emanations from it, and felt an urge to introduce it to the power centre. The result was astonishing. With the amulet on its side placed at the centre of the spiral, an immediate, precise energy manifestation was induced in the shape of the eight toothed 'cog' illustrated below—approximately 130 cm in diameter.

I dowsed it carefully many times, with three witnesses looking on, and marked the outline on the carpet with masking tape so that I could take accurate measurements. I was very excited by the positive nature of the response, and on impulse turned the amulet face downwards to see if there was any difference in the reaction. Immediately a second shape, more complicated than the first but just as positive, manifested as I dowsed. The twelve-petalled glyph was difficult to pin down accurately, but eventually we recorded the outline below.

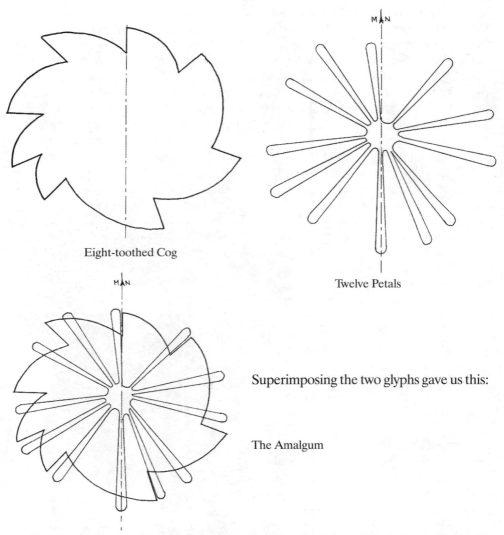

Eight-toothed Cog

Twelve Petals

Superimposing the two glyphs gave us this:

The Amalgum

The mandala created a strange feeling of familiarity and a stirring of residual memory, and I have asked for feedback from academic and otherwise inspired sources on its possible meaning or significance. The fact that there *is* a response from an otherwise innocent earth energy centre to such an artifact is in itself a thought-provoking phenomenon with awesome implications.

THE CRYSTAL SKULL

The amulet was not unique and I have since dowsed many intriguing stones and objects to see how the centre responds to their energy. There is so far no way of predicting whether there will be a positive reaction or whether the age of the artefact has any significant bearing on the result. Some of the ancient, authenticated items which looked most promising had no effect whatsoever, and some innocuous pieces triggered dramatic changes. Recently a number of people, pamphlets, publicity and periodicals seemed to launch a concerted attempt to get the Anna Mitchell-Hedges crystal skull into my mind. The universe patently required it to happen and while I have not yet been able to work with the skull itself, a good friend turned up quite by chance (!) with an excellent photograph.

Ba and I had a meditation with the energy centre to let her know what we proposed to do, then Ba left so that she could dowse later without any inkling of what I had found. As I introduced the photograph the rods almost leapt out of my hands as the energy from the centre powered them round in a tightening spiral.

The Crystal Skull

With the photograph in place the coloured skull gradually seemed to become three-dimensional and everything went very quiet. I had the feeling of an intake of breath, of time stopping, then a slow exhale as the full energy pattern started to manifest. I was very confused at first because every time I picked up a reaction it seemed to lead me back to the photograph. Slowly I became aware of a positive configuration, and as I dowsed it became more crisp and clearly defined. Six overlapping circles, approximately sixty centimetres in diameter, evenly spaced round the centre, were the first positive imprints. There was much more going on further out from the centre, but I wanted some confirmation of what I had found and asked Ba to dowse in her own way. I left the room, stunned by my first impressions of the manifestation, and waited patiently as Ba tuned in and went to work. When I went back she looked at me and said very softly ...

"It's the Seed of Life."

The Seed of Life

My heart sang; I had hardly dared hope that my interpretation would be confirmed. I dowsed again and even in that short time the basic six circles had expanded to ninety centimeters in diameter. The glyph is the centre part of the Flower of Life depicted on the walls of the ancient Osirion temple in Abydos, ninety miles from Luxor in Egypt. In *Awakening to Zero Point : the Collective Initiation*, Gregg Braden describes how this sacred geometric symbol was flash-burned into the stone structure of the temple more than ten thousand years ago with a technology we still don't understand. It is described as the lattice of pure life force, the ultimate code of creation.

The Flower of Life

We were humbled as we finished dowsing this extraordinary response from the earth. The nineteen circles are there. The pattern is in the global consciousness, in the fabric of the cosmos, and will inspire us humans on our pilgrimage to reach an understanding of our rightful place in the universe.

BOOK LIST

One precious gift we have is the freedom to spend time with our own choice of books.

There is a bewildering array available on every subject, and you can find the right ones by tuning into your inner needs. You will be astonished how often they just happen to fall into your lap.

Below are a few which, over the years, have had a pretty profound effect on my thinking, and may provide leads to help in your particular quest.

The Intelligent Universe .... Fred Hoyle
Winds of Change .... Julie Soskin
The Dance of the Wu Li Masters .... Gary Zukav
Dowsing Techniques and Applications ..... Tom Graves
Needles of Stone .... Tom Graves
The Chakras .... C.W.Leadbeater
The Psychic Power of Plants .... John Whitman
Living Water (Schauberger) .... Olaf Alex Andersson
Songlines .... Bruce Chatwin
Secret Shrines .... Paul Broadhurst
A New View over Atlantis .... John Michell
Dimensions of Paradise .... John Michell
Twelve Tribe Nations .... John Michell and Christine Rhone
Spiritual Dowsing .... Sig Lonegren
The Awakening Earth .... Peter Russell
The Quantum Society .... Danah Zohar and Ian Marshall
Pooh and the Ancient Mysteries .... John Tyerman Williams
Adam, Eve, and the Serpent .... Elaine Pagels
The Silent Road .... Wellesley Tudor Pole
The Prophet .... Kahlil Gibran
The Tao of Physics .... Fritjof Capra.

Magazines worthy of a browse to find one which suits you include Kindred Spirit, Resurgence, Caduceus, Nexus, Quest and New Humanity.

Earth Matters (Friends of the Earth), Trees are News (International Tree Foundation) World Wildlife Fund, Greenpeace, RSPB (Birdlife International), are amongst the higher profile organisations which work actively to improve our relationship with Mother Earth. From Positive News through Local Exchange Trading Systems to the hundreds of local groups concerned with caring for people and our environment, your energy input is their life blood, and will actively help to improve our lot.

DOWSING. Information from The British Society of Dowsers, Sycamore Barn, Tamley Lane, Hastingleigh, Ashford, Kent TN25 5HW. The quarterly Members' Journal has excellent articles on all aspects of dowsing.

DOWSING RODS. From author, PO BOX 11, Hayle, Cornwall TR27 6YF

INDEX